EASY TO COOK

PUDDINGS

Lyn Rutherford

BROCKHAMPTON PRESS
LONDON

First published in Great Britain in 1993 by
Anaya Publishers Ltd,
Strode House, 44–50 Osnaburgh Street, London NW1 3ND

This edition published 1996 by Brockhampton Press,
a member of Hodder Headline PLC Group

Design and art direction by Patrick McLeavey & Partners, London

Photographer: Patrick McLeavey
Home Economists: Meg Jansz, Lyn Rutherford and Annie Nichols
Photographic Stylists: Sue Storey, Marian Price
Editor: Gina Steer

British Library Cataloguing in Publication Data
Rutherford, Lyn
Easy to cook puddings. – (Easy to cook)

ISBN 1 86019 245 9

Typeset by Bookworm Typesetting, Manchester
Colour reproduction by Scantrans Pte Ltd, Singapore
Printed in UK by BPC Paulton Books Ltd

NOTES
Ingredients are listed in metric, imperial and cup
measurements.
Use one set of quantities as they are not
interchangeable.

All spoon measures are level:
1 tablespoon = one 15ml spoon
1 teaspoon = one 5ml spoon.

Use fresh herbs and freshly ground black pepper
unless otherwise stated.

Use standard size 3 eggs unless otherwise
suggested.

Throughout this book 'Preparation time' refers to the time required
to prepare the ingredients. It does not include time for cooking,
soaking, marinading etc, which is given in the recipe method.

CONTENTS

It may be a homely and comforting crumble or a rich warm tart in a thick blanket of creamy custard on a wintry day; it may be a midsummer delight of blazing red fruits, a sparkling sorbet or a dream of a chocolate concoction. Whatever your own favourite indulgence, there is always the perfect pudding for every occasion.

Easy To Cook Puddings contains recipes to suit all occasions. The *Fast And Simple* chapter has lots of delicious puddings that can be whipped up in just a few minutes – no standing or chilling or setting required. Try *Quick Grilled Papaya*, *Forest Fruit Platter*, classic *Soufflé Omelette* or *Liqueur Cheese Dip With Fruit Crudités*. In the *Light and Healthy* chapter there are pudding recipes to cheer the hearts of the strictest dieters and cholesterol watchers. *Irish Coffee Granita*, *Cheese Hearts with Fruit*, *Light Chocolate and Pear Dessert*, *Baked Bananas and Raspberry Yogurt Ice* amongst others prove that puddings don't have to be "just a moment on the lips, but a lifetime on the hips".

Everyone who loves puddings will know one or two *Traditional Favourites*. They may be remembered fondly from long ago or perhaps be among the many enjoying a revival in restaurants today. Included here are my special favourites, such as *Strawberry Shortcakes*, *Crème Brûlée*, *Maple Walnut and Chocolate Ice Cream* and *Summer Pudding*. *Tarts and Tartlets* are always a popular pudding choice, made simple here by the use of quickly prepared or ready made pastries plus ideas for delicious fillings and glazes which are easy to assemble. Be tempted by *Blueberry Franzipan Flan*, *Strawberry Boats*, *Filo Tartlets* and *Normandy Apple Flan*. Finally, there is a collection of puddings special enough for the grandest occasion and the most discerning diners. *Grand Puddings* such as *Chocolate and Vanilla Ice Cream Gâteau*, *Mille Feuilles*, *Meringue and Fruit Pyramid*

and *Vanilla Sponge with Strawberries and Cream* are stunning yet simple and taste as good as they look.

It's easy to be creative with puddings. The raw ingredients themselves are infinitely inspiring. There are fabulous fruits from all over the globe, sugars, scented honeys and fruit liqueurs to sweeten and flavour and herbs and flowers to impart their clean fresh flavours and perfumes. Chocolate comes sweet and creamy or dark and quite bitter, turning glossy, rich and smooth when melted. Dairy products such as soft cheeses, soured creams and yogurts complement and enrich any pudding, and pastries either short and crumbling or with light layers of crisp flakiness are the perfect contrast for sweet fillings. Such ingredients lend themselves beautifully to making simply delicious desserts.

In all cooking the quality of ingredients is of the utmost importance. You can only expect to achieve successful results and produce delicious dishes if the raw ingredients are to a good standard. This ever important rule is no less significant because the theme of this book is simple, easy to cook recipes. Simple dishes rely wholly on the quality of their ingredients, perhaps even more so than elaborate dishes where the true quality and freshness of the ingredients may be more easily disguised. The following notes will explain the uses of some of the ingredients and how to look for quality.

CHOCOLATE

There are a huge variety of chocolate bars on sale and if chocolate is all you desire I would always suggest you go for whatever is your favourite treat. However, for good results in cooking you need a good quality chocolate with a high percentage of cocoa solids. Read the backs of the wrappers to glean this information. Good quality chocolate is of the plain, dark variety, having more cocoa solids, and therefore a lower percentage of sugar. If your taste buds cry out for a sweeter flavour you can easily increase the sugar quantity in recipes such as mousses, ice creams and sauces but do not alter the proportions of a cake recipe or roulade, for example. Creamy milk chocolate, with careful melting, will be fine for coating purposes but will not give a good flavour in recipes. Choose chocolate with at least 50 per cent cocoa solids. This should be easy to find as many supermarkets now stock chocolate with around 70 per cent among their baking ingredients.

For white chocolate recipes avoid 'white chocolate flavoured bars' which are not the real thing at all and will not melt successfully but will separate into an oily mass.

EGGS
Egg whites will whisk better when the eggs are at room temperature and older eggs will give a better volume than those which are very fresh. Ensure bowl and beaters are clean as the merest amount of fat, even a tiny amount of yolk, will prevent the whites from foaming.

CRÈME FRAÎCHE
This is French soured cream and is richer than the soured cream produced in some other countries. It is thick, velvety and ideal for serving with many kinds of dessert. If you can't get it, a mixture of soured cream and thick double cream will make a good substitute.

FROMAGE FRAIS
This is a soft white cheese with the texture of thick yogurt. You can buy several versions with a fat content varying from 0 per cent to 8 per cent or even a creamy 40 per cent. The fat free or low fat varieties are great for calorie and cholesterol counters and can be used like yogurt in fools, mousses and cheesecakes.

MASCARPONE
This cream cheese comes from Italy and has a very high butterfat content. As you might expect, it is delicious, creamy and rich. You can buy it from Italian stores or in tubs in larger supermarkets. Use it sparingly, as a luxurious treat, to serve with desserts. You can substitute thick double cream but no other product is quite the same.

NUTS
We all know it's best to buy nuts in the shell and to crack them ourselves, but it is not really practical advice for cooking. Shelled nuts do not have a long shelf life and will quickly become rancid because of their high oil content. Buy them from shops with a fast turnover of sales and buy in small quantities as needed. They store better in the fridge than in a kitchen cupboard.

To toast nuts either grill them, turning frequently so they do not scorch, or brown in a moderately hot oven for 10–15 minutes.

ESSENCES AND EXTRACTS
Whenever possible, always buy pure essences and extracts. The essences of vanilla and almond are good examples of the 'real thing'! Avoid those labelled with the words "artificial" or "flavouring" as these are chemical substitutes and will not give a good true flavour at all.

Finally, eat and enjoy your puddings. I hope they inspire you to experiment and devise creations of your own. You can make even the simplest pudding a treat to eat by decorating with flowers, herbs, clusters of fruit, leaves and blossoms.

Go over the top and indulge yourself!

– 1 –
FAST AND SIMPLE

FOREST FRUIT PLATTER

INGREDIENTS

150 ml (¼ pint/ ⅔ cup) double
(thick) cream
1-2 tablespoons vanilla sugar
115g (4 oz/1 cup) raspberries
175g (6 oz/1¼ cup) blackberries
175g (6 oz/1¼ cup) small
strawberries
115g (4 oz/ ¾ cup) blueberries
4-6 tablespoon crème de cassis
To decorate: fruit leaves (optional)

METHOD   **Preparation time:** 10 minutes

In a small jug stir together the cream and sugar until the cream is slightly thickened. Pour onto four individual serving plates and tilt each plate to coat the base with cream.

Arrange the fruits on the cream, halving the strawberries if large - spoon the crème de cassis over the fruits or drizzle on to the cream if preferred.

Serve at once decorated with fruit leaves if liked.

VARIATION:
A lighter version, lower in calories, can be made by substituting most of the cream with natural low fat yogurt.

Serves 4

BAKED PEACHES WITH MASCARPONE

INGREDIENTS

25g (1 oz/2 tablespoons) butter, plus
extra for greasing
4 large ripe peaches
3 pieces stem ginger preserved in
syrup, plus syrup for basting
2 tablespoons caster sugar
150 ml (¼ pint/⅔ cup) sweet dessert
wine
25g (1 oz/2 tablespoons) flaked
almonds
To serve: mascarpone cheese and
fresh mint sprigs

METHOD   Preparation time: 5–10 minutes

Preheat the oven to 180° C/350° F
/Gas 4. Lightly grease an ovenproof
dish with butter. Ensure the dish is
large enough to take the 8 peach
halves in one layer.

Halve and stone the peaches and
place cut side up in the baking dish.
Finely dice the stem ginger and
sprinkle over the peaches with 2-3
tablespoons of the syrup from the jar.

Dot the peaches with the butter and
sprinkle with caster sugar. Pour the
wine into the dish and bake in the
preheated oven for about 20 minutes
until tender. Sprinkle the almonds
over the baked peaches and serve
warm or chilled with mascarpone
cheese, decorated with fresh mint
sprigs.

Serves 4

CITRUS CRÊPES

INGREDIENTS

Crêpes:
115g (4 oz/ ½ cup) plain flour
pinch of salt
1 egg, beaten
300 ml (½ pint/1¼ cups) semi-
  skimmed milk
1 tablespoon oil, plus extra for
  cooking
55g (2 oz/¼ cup) butter
55g (2 oz/¼ cup) caster sugar
pared rind and juice of 2 small
  oranges
pared rind and juice of 1 lemon
3 tablespoons Grand Marnier

METHOD

Preparation time: 30 minutes

To make the crêpe batter, sift the flour and salt into a large bowl. Make a well in the centre and drop in the egg. Gradually add the milk, beating with a wire whisk until smooth. Stir in the oil. Alternatively, to save time, put the ingredients in a blender or food processor and blend until smooth. Transfer the batter to a jug and leave to stand for 15 minutes before using.

Heat an omelette pan and add a few drops of oil. Pour in a little of the batter - just enough to thinly coat the base of the pan-tilting the pan as you do. Cook for about 30 seconds, until the underside is browned, then turn the crêpe and continue cooking for a few seconds only to set. Fold into quarters and transfer to a plate in a warm place to keep hot while cooking the rest of the crêpes. Continue making thin crêpes in this way until all the batter is used up.

Melt the butter in a large frying pan. Add the sugar, orange and lemon rinds and juices and bring to the boil. Add the cooked crêpes to the sauce and heat through for about 30 seconds. Lift the crêpes to a serving plate. Add the Grand Marnier to the pan and ignite. When the flames subside, pour the sauce over the crêpes and serve immediately.

Serves 4

INGREDIENTS

4 eggs, separated
2 tablespoons single (light) cream
2 teaspoons caster sugar
small pinch of salt
15g (½ oz/1 tablespoon) butter
3 tablespoons strawberry jam,
  preferably home-made
icing sugar, for sifting

METHOD

Preparation time: 10–12 minutes

Put the egg yolks in a mixing bowl with the cream and sugar and beat well. In a separate bowl whisk the egg whites with the salt until stiff. Lightly fold into the yolk mixture using a large metal spoon.

Preheat the grill to hot and set aside a plate to warm. Melt the butter in a large omelette pan, then pour in the egg mixture, spreading evenly. Cook on a medium heat for about 2 minutes until the base is set and lightly browned. Put the pan under the hot grill for 2-3 minutes until the top is well risen and set.

Meanwhile, heat the jam in a small saucepan and heat 2 metal skewers on the hob until glowing. Spread the jam over the omelette and fold in half. Quickly sift icing sugar over the top. Slide onto a heated plate and scorch the top with a lattice pattern using the hot skewers. Cut in half and serve immediately.

Serves 2

RUM BANANAS

INGREDIENTS

4 medium bananas
55g (2 oz/¼ cup) butter
*55g (2 oz/¼ cup) light soft brown
  sugar*
4 tablespoons dark rum
To decorate: toasted almond flakes
*To serve: whipped cream or ice
  cream*

METHOD **Preparation time:** 6–8 minutes

Peel the bananas and using a sharp knife cut in half lengthwise. Melt the butter in a large frying pan, add the bananas and cook for 3 minutes, turning carefully with a wooden spoon or spatula.

Sprinkle over the sugar and stir in gently. Continue cooking, stirring occasionally for about 2 minutes until the bananas are just tender.

Add the rum to the pan and bring to the boil. Immediately set alight. When the flames subside serve at once, sprinkled with toasted almond flakes and whipped cream or scoops of ice cream.

Serves 4

INGREDIENTS

2 papayas
juice of 1 lime
4 tablespoons caster sugar
1-2 teaspoons ground ginger
To serve: crème fraîche or ice cream

METHOD   Preparation time: 15 minutes

Preheat the grill to hot. Cut the papayas in half lengthwise and scoop out and discard the seeds. Cut each piece in half lengthwise to give eight quarters. Arrange flesh side up on a baking tray or in a shallow heat-proof dish.

Sprinkle the lime juice over the papaya flesh. In a small bowl or cup mix together the caster sugar and ground ginger. Sprinkle over the papaya.

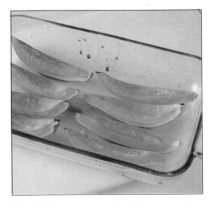

Cook the papaya under the hot grill for a few minutes until the sugar begins to caramelize. Serve immediately or cooled slightly with crème fraîche or ice cream.

Serves 4

INGREDIENTS

Sauce:
1 large ripe mango
juice of ½ lemon
2 teaspoons honey
Kebabs:
1 ripe pear, cored and cut into
*   wedges*
1 nectarine, stoned and cut into
*   wedges*
2 large plums or greengages, stoned
*   and quartered*
8 large strawberries
1 banana, peeled and cut into chunks
45g (1½ oz/2½ tablespoons)
*   unsalted butter*
2 tablespoons caster sugar
juice of ½ lemon

METHOD

Preparation time: 25 minutes

To prepare the sauce, peel the mango and cut all the flesh away from the stone. Roughly chop the flesh and place in a blender or food processor with the lemon juice and honey. Process until smooth. Transfer to a bowl, cover and chill until required.

For the kebabs, preheat the grill just before you are ready to serve the kebabs. Thread the prepared fruit on to 8 small wooden skewers, alternating the fruits and dividing equally.

Melt the butter in a small saucepan and stir in the sugar and lemon juice. Brush half of the mixture over the kebabs and cook them under a hot grill for 2-3 minutes, turning and brushing with the remaining mixture halfway through. Serve immediately with the mango sauce.

Serves 4

FRESH FIGS WITH HONEY AND YOGURT

INGREDIENTS

*450g (1 lb/1 cup) fresh ripe purple
  or green figs*
3 tablespoons clear honey
2 teaspoons lemon or orange juice
*250 ml (8 fl oz/1 cup) thick Greek
  yogurt*
*2 teaspoons finely chopped fresh
  mint*
To decorate: mint sprigs

METHOD

Preparation time: 10 minutes

Peel the figs and using a small sharp kitchen knife cut into quarters or slices. Arrange in one layer on a serving platter or individual plates.

Mix together the honey and lemon or orange juice and drizzle over the figs. Cover loosely with clingfilm and chill in the fridge for about 30 minutes or until ready to serve.

Just before serving, spoon the yogurt over the figs and sprinkle with the chopped fresh mint. Serve decorated with mint sprigs.

Serves 4

LIQUEUR CHEESE DIP WITH FRUIT CRUDITÉS

INGREDIENTS

350g (12 oz/1½ cups) cream cheese
*150 ml (¼ pint/⅔ cup) whipping
  cream*
*4 tablespoons Grand Marnier, or
  other fruit liqueur*
2 eggs
*25g (1 oz/2 tablespoons) caster
  sugar*
Fruit crudités:
  *prepared ripe fruits such as
  strawberries, wedges of peach
  and nectarine, physalis, pear slices,
  halves of apricot or plum and soft
  berries such as raspberries and
  blackberries when available on
  the stalk.*
  dessert biscuits
*To decorate: pared orange zest or
  fruit leaves*

METHOD   **Preparation time:** 30 minutes

Mix together the cream cheese, whipping cream and Grand Marnier in a bowl until smooth. In a large separate bowl whisk the eggs and sugar until light and fluffy. Fold in the cheese mixture using a metal spoon.

Transfer the dip to a serving dish or individual glasses and chill until required. Meanwhile prepare the fruit crudités and arrange on a platter or individual plates.

Serve the liqueur cheese, decorated with pared orange zest or fruit leaves, with the prepared fruit and dessert biscuits for dipping.

Serves 4

STRAWBERRY FRITTERS

INGREDIENTS

Batter:
55g (2 oz/¼ cup) plain flour
pinch of salt
1 tablespoon caster sugar
2 eggs, separated
3 tablespoons milk
450g (1 lb/4 cups) small
  strawberries
oil for deep frying
vanilla sugar, for dredging
To serve: lightly whipped cream

METHOD

Preparation time: 30 minutes

Sift the flour and salt into a large bowl. Stir in the sugar, then add the egg yolks and milk and beat well to form a smooth batter. Set aside. Hull the strawberries and wipe clean but do not wash. Heat the oil for deep frying. In a clean bowl whisk the egg whites until fairly stiff and fold into the batter. Drop the strawberries into the batter.

Dip a large metal spoon into the hot oil, then use to spoon three or four coated strawberries into the hot oil. Fry for about 2 minutes, turning once until golden and then drain on kitchen paper. Repeat in small batches until all the strawberries are done. Serve the hot fritters dredged generously with vanilla sugar and with lightly whipped cream to accompany.

VANILLA SUGAR
To make vanilla sugar, simply place one or two vanilla pods in a jar with a tight fitting lid and fill the jar with caster sugar. Store and the sugar will become scented and flavoured by the vanilla. You can top up the sugar at any time and can also use the vanilla pods for other recipes and then wash and dry thoroughly and return to the jar.

Serves 4

INGREDIENTS

350g (12 oz/2 ½ cups) soft fruit eg strawberries, raspberries or blackberries
55g (2 oz/¼ cup) caster or vanilla sugar
150 ml (¼ pint/⅔ cup) fromage frais
150 ml (¼ pint/⅔ cup) double (thick) cream
To serve: crisp dessert biscuits

METHOD

Preparation time: 15 minutes

Set aside four whole fruit for decorating. Put the rest in a food processor or blender with the sugar and process until smooth. Push through a sieve into a bowl, to remove the seeds.

Stir in the fromage frais. Whip the cream until it stands in stiff peaks. Stir in a little of the fruit mixture to lighten and then fold into the rest of the fruit mixture.

Divide between four serving glasses and decorate with the reserved whole fruit. Serve at once with crisp dessert biscuits.

Serves 4

ZABAGLIONE

INGREDIENTS

4 egg yolks
55g (2 oz/¹⁄₄ cup) caster sugar
4 tablespoons Marsala wine
To serve: amaretti biscuits or sponge
  fingers

METHOD

Preparation time: 15 minutes

Place the egg yolks in a large bowl with the sugar and Marsala wine. Using an electric whisk on high speed, with the bowl set over a pan of simmering water, whisk for about 10 minutes until very thick and mousse-like.

Pour into four individual serving glasses and serve immediately with amaretti biscuits or sponge fingers.

VARIATION:
For a slightly tangy flavour add the finely grated rind of 1 small lemon. Add to the bowl at the start and whisk as above.

Serves 4

BAKED BANANAS

INGREDIENTS

4 medium bananas, unpeeled
To serve:
115g (4 oz/ ½ cup) Greek yogurt
4 teaspoons clear honey
½ teaspoon ground cinnamon

METHOD   Preparation time: 5 minutes

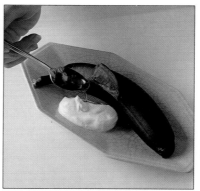

Preheat the oven to 200° C/ 400° F/Gas 6. Place the bananas, still in their skins, on a baking sheet and bake in the oven for 20-25 minutes until the skins are completely blackened.

Serve the bananas immediately on individual plates, each with a spoonful of Greek yogurt which is drizzled with honey and sprinkled with a little ground cinnamon.

Serves 4

HONEY
Honey is produced by bees from the nectar they take from flowers. The type of flower will affect the flavour and the purest flavours are obtained when the bees are fed on just one type of flower. These honeys are known as 'monofloral' and are a little more expensive than the blended variety. Good monofloral honeys which are fairly widely available are Acacia, Orange Blossom, Clover and Lavender. They all have wonderful flavours characteristic of the flower.

INGREDIENTS

225g (8 oz) full fat cream cheese
3 tablespoons double cream
2 ½ tablespoons vanilla sugar
1 egg, separated
225g (8 oz) summer fruit, such as
 blueberries, loganberries,
raspberries, strawberries etc
shortbread triangles

METHOD

Preparation time: 15 minutes

Put the cream cheese in a bowl with the double cream, vanilla sugar and egg yolk. Beat well with a wooden spoon until smooth.

In a separate bowl whisk the egg white until stiff. Using a large metal spoon fold into the cheese mixture.

Spoon the vanilla cheese onto four individual serving plates. Tumble the fruit over and around and serve each with shortbread triangles.

NOTE:
Vanilla sugar may be bought in sachets, or it is simple to make your own (see page 17). If it is not available for this recipe you can use caster sugar and ½ teaspoon natural vanilla essence, but the flavour will be less subtly scented.

Serves 4

BANANA AND PASSION FRUIT WHIP

INGREDIENTS

3 passion fruits
3 small ripe bananas
150 ml (¹/₄ pint) double cream
5 tablespoons fromage frais
To serve: crisp dessert biscuits

METHOD   **Preparation time:** 15 minutes

Halve the passion fruits. Scoop the seeds and juice of two fruits into a bowl. Peel two of the bananas and mash the flesh. Stir into the passion fruit pulp.

Whip the cream until soft peaks form and fold into the fruit with the fromage frais. Thinly slice the remaining banana and fold in.

Spoon the mixture into four serving glasses or bowls and top each with a little of the remaining passion fruit pulp. Serve at once with crisp dessert biscuits.

NOTE:
Passion fruit are ripest when they are wrinkliest, and the flavour will be much sweeter and more scented than those eaten when the fruits are smooth and round.

Serves 4

– 2 –
LIGHT AND HEALTHY

LIGHT CHEESE HEARTS WITH FRUIT

INGREDIENTS

175g (6 oz/³⁄₄ cup) cottage cheese
*175g (6 oz/³⁄₄ cup) fromage frais (8%
  fat)*
1 tablespoon caster sugar
¹⁄₂-1 teaspoon vanilla essence
2 egg whites
To serve:
*fresh fruits, eg 225g (8 oz 1¹⁄₂ cups)
  strawberries, halved*
*or 4 apricots, stoned and halved plus
  115g (4 oz/³⁄₄ cup) raspberries*
4 teaspoons clear honey

METHOD

Preparation time: 25 minutes

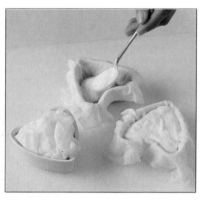

Line four perforated porcelain heart moulds with a double thickness of damp muslin. Stand on a tray or baking sheet and set aside. Sieve the cottage cheese into a bowl. Stir in the fromage frais, sugar and vanilla essence, and beat well with a wooden spoon.

Whisk the egg whites until fairly stiff and fold into the cheese mixture. Spoon into the prepared moulds, folding the edges of muslin over to cover. Chill overnight on the tray to catch the excess liquid.

To serve, unmould the cheese hearts onto individual serving plates and arrange the fruits around them. Spoon a little honey over the fruit.

Serves 4

INGREDIENTS

2 medium oranges
8 clementines
3 tablespoons clear honey
1-2 tablespoons orange flower water
To serve: Greek yogurt

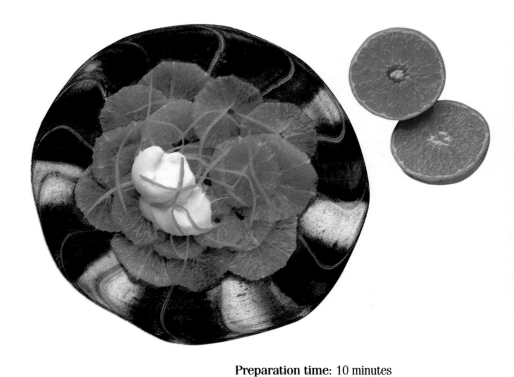

METHOD

Preparation time: 10 minutes

Using a sharp knife, thinly peel the rind from the two oranges. Cut the peel into long thin strips and blanch in a pan of boiling water for 30 seconds. Refresh in cold water, drain and set aside. With the knife cut away the pith from the oranges. Thinly slice the oranges and place in a bowl. Add the strips of orange zest.

Peel the clementines and slice as thinly as possible. Add to the bowl with the honey and stir well to mix. Chill for at least 30 minutes before serving.

Just before serving sprinkle with orange flower water. Stir the ingredients gently together, taking care not to break up the fruit. Serve with Greek yogurt.

Serves 4

RASPBERRY YOGURT ICE

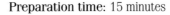

INGREDIENTS

350g (12 oz/2½ cups) fresh
  raspberries
3 tablespoons orange juice
85-115g (3-4 oz/⅓-½ cup) caster
  sugar, depending on sweetness
preferred
150 ml (¼ pint/⅔ cup) low-fat
  natural yogurt
175g (6 oz/¾ cup) Greek yogurt
1 egg white
To decorate: fresh raspberries and
  lemon balm sprigs

METHOD   **Preparation time:** 15 minutes

Set freezer to rapid freeze. Purée the raspberries using a blender or food processor, then sieve into a large bowl to remove the seeds. Stir in the orange juice and 55g (2 oz/¼ cup) of the sugar. Mix together the two yogurts and stir into the fruit purée. Whisk lightly to mix.

Whisk the egg white until stiff then whisk in the remaining sugar. Fold into the fruit mixture. Pour into a rigid freezer-proof container, cover and freeze for about 2 hours, until slushy.

Remove the yogurt ice from the freezer and whisk until smooth. This will break down large ice crystals. Cover and return to the freezer for at least 4 hours until firm. Remember to return freezer to normal setting.
To serve, allow to soften in the fridge for 15 minutes before scooping into chilled dishes. Serve with extra fresh raspberries and lemon balm sprigs to decorate.

Serves 4

ICED EXOTIC FRUITS

INGREDIENTS

crushed ice
8 lychees
1 papaya
1 peach or nectarine
1 star fruit
1 pomegranate
225g (8 oz/1½ cups) strawberries,
   halved, or 150g (5 oz/1 cup)
alpine strawberries
175g (6 oz/1¼ cups) raspberries
4-6 teaspoons orange flower water
To decorate: borage flowers
   (optional)

METHOD

Preparation time: 15 minutes

Pile crushed ice on to four individual serving plates or one large platter. Put in the freezer until required. Peel the lychees and the papaya and remove the stones and seeds. Dice the papaya flesh.

Stone and slice the peach or nectarine. Thinly slice the star fruit. Quarter the pomegranate and carefully remove the seeds to a small bowl, catching any juice.

About ten minutes before serving, arrange all the fruits on the crushed ice and sprinkle with the pomegranate juice and orange flower water. Top with borage flowers for extra decoration, if liked. Place each serving on a second plate to serve.

NOTE:
Crush ice by wrapping in a clean tea towel and pounding with a rolling pin or mallet.

Serves 4

CHILLED FRUIT SOUP

INGREDIENTS

2 ripe Ogen or Galia melons
3 tablespoons caster sugar
1 large orange
225g (8 oz/1½ cups) small
  strawberries, halved
To decorate: borage flowers,
  (optional)

METHOD   **Preparation time:** 15 minutes

Halve the melons and discard the seeds. Scoop the flesh into a blender or food processor. Add the sugar and blend until smooth. Transfer to a bowl and chill for at least 1 hour or until almost ready to serve.

Using a sharp knife cut away the skin and pith of the orange. Holding over a bowl to catch the juice, cut out the orange segments. Cut these in half and add to the melon, along with any juice.

To serve, place four serving bowls on plates and surround with crushed ice. Spoon the soup into each and divide the strawberries between them. Decorate with borage flowers, if liked.

Serves 4

CHARENTAIS FRUIT CUPS

INGREDIENTS

175g (6 oz/1 cup) small strawberries
225g (8 oz/1½ cups) raspberries
2 tablespoons caster sugar
3-4 tablespoons Grand Marnier or
  Cointreau
2 charentais melons or other orange
  fleshed melons
To decorate: fruit leaves, if available

METHOD

Preparation time: 15 minutes

Hull the strawberries and halve them. Place in a bowl with the raspberries and sprinkle over the caster sugar and liqueur. Toss lightly to mix, cover and chill for at least 1 hour, or up to 3 hours. Put the melons to chill at the same time.

As soon as possible before serving cut the melons in half and remove a thin slice from the base of each half so they do not topple. Scoop out and discard the melon seeds.

Divide the fruit mixture between the melon halves and serve decorated with fruit leaves, if available.

NOTE:
It is important to choose melons that are ripe and fragrant for this simple refreshing dessert.

Serves 4

INGREDIENTS

85g (3 oz/¹/₃ cup) soft brown sugar
600 ml (1 pint/2 cups) water
2 tablespoons instant coffee granules
6 tablespoons Irish whiskey
To decorate: 150 ml (¹/₄ pint/²/₃ cup)
  double (thick) cream (optional),
  cocoa powder

METHOD   Preparation time: 25 minutes

Set freezer to rapid freeze. Put the sugar and water in a medium saucepan and heat gently, stirring until the sugar is dissolved. Bring to the boil and allow to boil steadily for 5 minutes. Remove from the heat and stir in the instant coffee granules. Allow to cool.

When the coffee mixture is cold stir in the whiskey and transfer to a rigid freezer-proof container. Cover and freeze for about 2 hours until slushy. Remove the granita from the freezer and whisk to break up the ice crystals. Re-freeze as before. After 2 hours whisk again, cover and freeze until firm.

Ten minutes before serving, whip the cream, if using, until it forms soft peaks. Remove the granita from the freezer and allow to stand for 10 minutes at room temperature. Stir well until granular and spoon into tall stemmed serving glasses. If using, top each with a swirl of cream and dust lightly with cocoa powder. Remember to return freezer to normal setting.

Serves 4-6

LIGHT CHOCOLATE AND PEAR DESSERTS

INGREDIENTS

1 ripe pear
175g (6 oz/1¼ cup) raspberries
1 tablespoon caster sugar
1 x 225g (8 oz/1 cup) carton Greek
   yogurt
1 x 150 ml (5 fl oz/⅔ cup) carton
   natural yogurt
2 tablespoons cocoa powder, sifted
4 tablespoons icing sugar
To decorate: extra raspberries and
   mint sprigs

METHOD
Preparation time: 20 minutes

Peel and core the pear. Chop into small even pieces and place in a bowl with the raspberries. Sprinkle over the caster sugar and stir lightly to mix.

In a separate bowl whisk together the yogurts, cocoa powder and icing sugar until smooth. Spoon one third of the mixture into four individual serving glasses. Top this with half of the prepared fruit.

Continue layering the chocolate mixture and fruit, ending with a chocolate layer. Serve immediately, or lightly chilled, decorating each with extra raspberries and a mint sprig.

Serves 4

STRAWBERRY AND KIWI SALAD WITH YOGURT FROTH

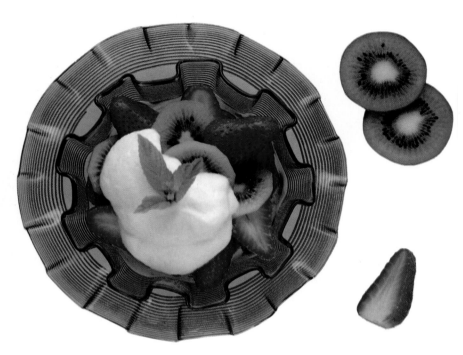

INGREDIENTS

2 kiwi fruits
350g (12 oz/2½ cups) strawberries
1 tablespoon icing sugar, sifted
Yogurt froth:
175g (6 oz/¾ cup) Greek yogurt
2 tablespoons Grand Marnier or
  kirsch
1 egg white
25g (1 oz/2 tablespoons) caster
  sugar
To decorate: mint sprigs or
  strawberry leaves

METHOD   **Preparation time:** 20 minutes

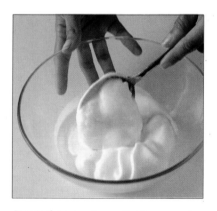

Peel the kiwi fruits using a small sharp knife or a vegetable peeler and cut into thin slices. Hull and halve the strawberries. Place all the fruit in a bowl and sprinkle over the icing sugar. Toss lightly to mix, cover and chill for at least 30 minutes and up to 3 hours.

Just before serving make the yogurt froth. In a large bowl mix together the Greek yogurt and liqueur. In a separate bowl whisk the egg white until stiff. Add the sugar and whisk again for a few seconds. Fold the egg white mixture into the yogurt mixture.

Serve the strawberry and kiwi salad immediately in individual serving dishes with the yogurt froth spooned over. Decorate with mint sprigs or strawberry leaves.

Serves 4

TROPICAL FRUIT SALAD

INGREDIENTS

1 small pineapple
2 guavas
2 tablespoons demerara sugar
juice of 1 lime
2 bananas
2 passion fruits
To decorate: fine strips of lime peel

METHOD

Preparation time: 15 minutes

Using a sharp kitchen knife, discard the plume and stalk end from the pineapple. Peel and cut into bite-sized pieces, discarding the woody central core. Peel the guavas and slice into thin wedges.

Put the pineapple chunks and guava slices into a large shallow dish and sprinkle over the sugar and lime juice. Toss lightly to mix and chill in the fridge for 30 minutes.

Peel the bananas and slice thickly. Add to the pineapple mixture and toss lightly. Halve the passion fruits and scoop out the flesh using a teaspoon. Spoon over the salad and serve at once, decorated with fine strips of lime peel.

Serves 4

INGREDIENTS

1 large ripe mango
3-4 tablespoons caster sugar
225 g (8 oz/1 cup) thick Greek
  yogurt
3 tablespoons orange juice
1 x 11g (½ oz/1 tablespoon) sachet
  powdered gelatine
1 egg white
4 passion fruit
To decorate: sprigs of mint or lemon
  balm

METHOD

Preparation time: 20–25 minutes

Lightly oil four individual pudding basins. Peel the mango and cut the flesh away from the stone. Chop roughly and place in a food processor or blender with 3 tablespoons caster sugar. Process until smooth. Transfer to a large bowl. Add the yogurt to the mango purée. Stir well and taste for sweetness, adding the extra tablespoon of sugar if preferred.

Put the orange juice in a small bowl or cup and sprinkle over the gelatine. Leave to soak for 1 minute then stand the bowl in a pan of hot water and stir until dissolved. Add to the yogurt mixture, stirring well. In a clean bowl, whisk the egg white until stiff. Using a large metal spoon, fold into the yogurt mixture. Spoon into the prepared pudding basins and chill for at least 1 hour until set.

To unmould the mango creams dip the moulds, one at a time, into warm water. Turn out on to individual serving plates. Cut the passion fruit in half and using a teaspoon scoop out the seeds and juice. Spoon over and around the mango creams. Decorate each with sprigs of mint or lemon balm.

Serves 4

INGREDIENTS

*115g (4 oz/1 cup) seedless green or
  red grapes*
*2 x 11g (1 oz/2 tablespoons) sachet
  powdered gelatine*
*450 ml (³/₄ pint/1³/₄ cups) freshly
  squeezed mandarin juice*
2-3 tablespoons sugar
*To decorate: mandarin orange slices
  and mint sprigs or small vine leaves*

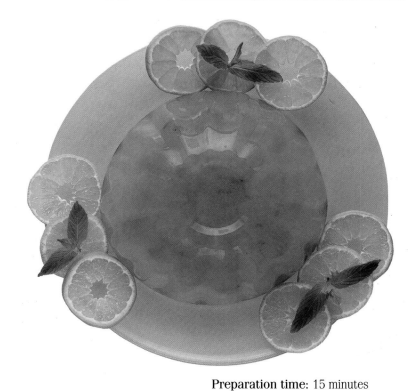

METHOD

Preparation time: 15 minutes

Halve the grapes and set aside. Pour
four tablespoons of cold water into a
small bowl and sprinkle the gelatine
over the surface. Leave for 2-3
minutes until spongy. Place the bowl
over a pan of hot water and stir until
completely dissolved.

Put the mandarin juice and sugar into
a saucepan with 300 ml (½ pint/1
cup) water. Bring to the boil, stirring
until the sugar is dissolved. Remove
from the heat and stir in the gelatine.
Strain into a jug and allow to cool
slightly.

Place the prepared grapes in a wetted
900 ml (1½ pint/2½ cups) mould.
Pour in the mandarin jelly liquid and
chill until set (about 2 hours). To
unmould, carefully dip the mould into
warm water and invert on to a
serving plate. Decorate with sliced
unpeeled mandarins and mint sprigs
or small vine leaves.

Serves 4

INGREDIENTS

225g (8 oz) frozen raspberries
350g (12 oz) frozen blackcurrants
3 tablespoons caster sugar
3 teaspoons powdered gelatine
6 tablespoons orange juice
To serve: Greek or low-fat natural
  yogurt sweetened with a little honey
To decorate: mint leaves

METHOD   **Preparation time:** 15 minutes

Put the raspberries and blackcurrants into separate bowls and leave to defrost completely. Add one tablespoon sugar to the raspberries and two to the blackcurrants. Stir well and mash the fruits slightly with a fork to break up. In a small bowl or cup soak half the gelatine in 3 tablespoons of orange juice. Stand in a saucepan of simmering water and stir until dissolved. Stir into the raspberries.

Divide the raspberries between four dariole moulds. They should almost half fill them. Chill for 20-30 minutes until lightly set. Soak the remaining gelatine in the rest of the orange juice and dissolve as before. Stir into the blackcurrants. Spoon the mixture into the dariole moulds to fill completely, and chill for at least 1½ hours until set.

To unmould, dip the dariole moulds, one at a time, into hot water for a few seconds then invert on to a serving plate. Serve with Greek or low-fat yogurt sweetened with a little honey and decorate each serving with mint leaves.

Serves 4

BAKED APPLES WITH APRICOT AND COCONUT

INGREDIENTS

55g (2 oz) no soak dried apricots
25g (1 oz) sultanas or raisins
3 tablespoons dessicated coconut
3 tablespoons soft light brown sugar
½ teaspoon ground cinnamon
4 large cooking apples
To serve: thick set yogurt or fromage
  frais

METHOD   Preparation time: 15 minutes

Preheat the oven to 180° C/350° F/
Gas 4. Finely chop the apricots and
place in a bowl with the sultanas or
raisins, coconut, sugar and cinnamon.
Mix well.

Remove the cores from the apples.
Using a small sharp knife, make a
shallow cut around the middle of
each. Stand the apples in an
ovenproof dish.

Use the apricot mixture to fill the
apples, pressing in as firmly as
possible. Spoon four tablespoons
water around. Bake in the oven for
40-50 minutes until soft. Serve hot
with thick set yogurt or fromage frais.

Serves 4

PAPAYA AND HONEY FROMAGE FRAIS

INGREDIENTS

2 ripe papayas
1 tablespoon clear honey
225g (8 oz) fromage frais
8 ratafia or 4 amaretti biscuits
  (optional)
To decorate: mint sprigs

METHOD   Preparation time: 10 minutes

Halve the papayas and scoop out and discard the black seeds. Scoop the flesh from three of the halves into a food processor or blender, add the honey and blend until smooth. Transfer to a bowl.

Chop the flesh of the remaining papaya half. Stir the fromage frais into the fruit purée and then fold in the chopped fruit.

Spoon the mixture into four serving glasses and chill for at least 20 minutes before serving with ratafia or amaretti biscuits, if liked. Decorate with mint sprigs.

NOTE:
Try crumbling the amaretti biscuits in the base of the serving glasses before spooning in the fruit fromage frais.

Serves 4

– 3 –
TRADITIONAL FAVOURITES

TIRAMISU

INGREDIENTS

1 teaspoon instant coffee granules
4 tablespoons Marsala wine
8 tablespoons brandy
8 sponge fingers, halved
6 amaretti biscuits
350g (12 oz/1½ cups) mascarpone
  cheese
3 eggs, separated
55g (2 oz/¼ cup) caster sugar
85g (3 oz/⅓ cup) plain (dark)
  chocolate, grated

METHOD   **Preparation time:** 30 minutes

In a shallow bowl dissolve the instant coffee in 2 tablespoons boiling water. Stir in the Marsala wine and brandy. Dip the sponge fingers into the mixture and arrange in the bottom of a glass serving dish or individual serving glasses. Crumble the amaretti biscuits over.

Put the mascarpone cheese into a bowl and stir well. Put the egg yolks and sugar in a large bowl. Using a whisk, beat until pale and thick. Stir a little into the mascarpone cheese, to lighten, then gradually add the mascarpone mixture to the egg yolks, whisking well between each addition. In a separate bowl whisk the egg whites until stiff and fold into the cheese mixture using a large metal spoon. Pour half of the mixture over the sponge fingers.

Sprinkle most of the chocolate in a layer over the surface of the cheese then cover with the remaining mixture, smoothing the surface. Cover and chill overnight. Just before serving, sprinkle the remaining chocolate over the surface of the pudding.

Serves 6

SYLLABUB

INGREDIENTS

*finely grated rind and juice of 1
lemon*
*125 ml (4 fl oz/½ cup) sweet dessert
wine such as Moscatel de Valencia*
*300 ml (½ pint/1¼ cups) double
(thick) cream*
70g (2½ oz/¼ cup) caster sugar
1 egg white
*To serve: crisp dessert biscuits such
as almond tuilles or langues de chat*

METHOD

Preparation time: 15 minutes

In a small jug mix together the lemon rind and juice and the dessert wine. Cover and leave to stand for 15 minutes to allow flavours to infuse.

In a large bowl whip the cream with about half of the sugar until it forms stiff peaks then stir in the wine mixture and whip again until the mixture holds its shape.

Whisk the egg white until stiff. Add the remaining sugar and whisk again lightly. Fold into the cream mixture using a large metal spoon. Divide the mixture between four serving glasses and serve at once, or lightly chilled, with crisp dessert biscuits.

Serves 4

STRAWBERRY SHORTCAKES

INGREDIENTS

Sauce:
225g (8 oz/1½ cups) strawberries,
  hulled
1 tablespoon caster sugar
2 tablespoons orange juice
Shortcakes:
175g (6 oz/¾ cup) plain flour
115g (4 oz/½ cup) unsalted butter,
  softened
55g (2 oz/¼ cup) caster sugar, plus
  extra for rolling out
To serve:
300 ml (½ pint/1¼ cups) double
  (thick) cream
175g (6 oz/1 cup) alpine
  strawberries, or small strawberries,
  halved
icing sugar, for dusting

METHOD   **Preparation time:** 30 minutes

To make the sauce put the strawberries, sugar and orange juice into a blender or food processor and purée until smooth. Sieve into a bowl or jug and chill until required.

Preheat the oven to 150° C/300° F/ Gas 2. For the shortcakes, grease two baking sheets and line with baking parchment. Sieve the flour into a bowl and rub in the butter. Add the sugar and work to a stiff paste using your hands. Turn onto a surface lightly dusted with caster sugar.

Roll out the shortcake paste to 5mm (¼ inch) thickness. Use a 8.5 cm (3½ inch) metal cutter to stamp out 6 rounds. Re-roll the trimmings and use a 5 cm (2 inch) cutter to stamp out 6 smaller rounds.

Lay the two sizes of shortcake rounds on separate baking sheets. Chill for 10 minutes, then bake in the preheated oven for 25-30 minutes until lightly coloured and crisp. Cool on wire racks.

To assemble the shortcakes, whip the cream until it forms soft peaks. Spoon or pipe over the larger shortcakes. Transfer to individual serving plates and divide the strawberries between them, arranging them on top of the cream.

Place the small shortcakes on top of the larger bases and dust each with a little icing sugar. Just before serving, pool a little of the reserved strawberry sauce around each shortcake.

Serves 6

VARIATION

BRAMBLE SHORTCAKES WITH RASPBERRY SAUCE
Substitute 225g (8 oz/1½ cup) raspberries for the strawberries in the sauce and use 175g (6 oz/1 cup) fresh blackberries in the filling.

NOTE:
The shortcakes and sauce can both be prepared ahead and assembled at the last minute. Store the shortcakes in an airtight tin.

Left: as a delicious variation substitute blackberries for strawberries and use a raspberry sauce, shown here feathered with cream.

STRAWBERRY AND ORANGE TRIFLE

INGREDIENTS

Thick custard:
3 egg yolks
45g (1½ oz/2½ tablespoons) caster sugar
½ teaspoon vanilla essence
2 tablespoons cornflour
450 ml (¾ pint/scant 2 cups) milk
4 trifle sponge cakes
4 tablespoons strawberry jam
2 oranges, peeled and segmented
12 ratafias
½ teaspoon finely grated orange zest
4 tablespoons Grand Marnier
350g (12 oz/2½ cups) small fresh strawberries
450 ml (¾ pint/scant 2 cups) double (thick) cream
To decorate: strawberry leaves or mint sprigs

METHOD

Preparation time: 25 minutes

First make the custard. In a large bowl mix together the egg yolks, sugar, vanilla essence and cornflour. Heat the milk in a saucepan to almost boiling then pour over the egg mixture stirring well. Return the mixture to the pan and cook gently stirring throughout, until thickened. Transfer back to the bowl and allow to cool completely, covered closely with a layer of clingfilm to prevent a skin forming.

Cut the trifle sponges in half. Spread one half with the strawberry jam and sandwich the cakes back together. Arrange in the bottom of a glass serving dish with the orange segments. Crumble the ratafias and sprinkle over with the orange zest. Spoon over the Grand Marnier. Reserve some whole strawberries for decoration, then halve the rest and arrange in the dish. Spread the cold custard over the sponges and fruit to cover completely. Chill until lightly set.

Whip the cream until it forms soft peaks and use half to cover the trifle. Use the remaining cream to decorate the trifle with the reserved strawberries, leaves or mint sprigs. Chill for 1 hour before serving.

Serves 6

SUMMER PUDDING

INGREDIENTS

450g (1 lb/4 cups) raspberries, or a
  mixture of raspberries and
  blackberries, hulled
115g (4 oz/½ cup) caster sugar
450g (1 lb/4 cups) fresh mixed
  currants (red, black and white)
8-10 large slices thinly cut white
  bread
To decorate: fruit leaves and sprigs of
  currants
To serve: whipped cream or thick
  yogurt

METHOD

Preparation time: 30 minutes

Put the raspberries and blackberries,
if using, in a large bowl with 55g (2
oz/¼ cup) of the sugar. Stir lightly
and leave for 2-3 hours, until the
juices run. Pick over the currants,
removing stalks. Place in a saucepan
with the remaining sugar and 2
tablespoons of water. Heat gently for
3-4 minutes, stirring frequently until
the fruit is tender but not pulpy.
Remove from the heat and allow to
cool.

Add the currants to the berries and
mix gently. Taste for sweetness at this
stage and add a little more sugar if
necessary. The exact amount required
depends on the sweetness of the fruits.
Remove the crusts from the bread, and
reserve 3 slices. Use remaining bread
to line the base and sides of a 900 ml
(1½ pint/3 cup) pudding basin,
overlapping the bread. Spoon the fruit
into the basin, soaking the bread with
the juices. Cover with the reserved
bread slices and if any surplus juices
remain, spoon these over.

Cover the bowl with a small plate and
place a weight on top. Chill overnight.
To unmould and serve remove small
plate and weight then place a serving
plate upside down on top of the
pudding. Invert both together and
carefully lift off the basin. Decorate
with fruit leaves and currants.

Serves 6-8

CRÈME BRÛLÉE WITH FRESH FRUITS

INGREDIENTS
....

4 egg yolks
85g (3 oz/¹/₃ cup) caster sugar
1 teaspoon vanilla essence
600 ml (1 pint/2¹/₂ cups) double
  (thick) cream
To serve: fresh fruits in season such
  as summer berries and apricots or
  winter clementines and physalis

METHOD   **Preparation time:** 20 minutes

Preheat the oven to 150° C/300°F/ Gas 2. In a large mixing bowl beat together the egg yolks, 45g (1½ oz/ 2½ tablespoons) of the sugar and the vanilla essence. Heat the cream in a small saucepan until almost boiling. Pour over the egg yolks, beating with a wire whisk at the same time. Place the bowl over a pan of simmering water and whisk lightly until the mixture thickens to coat the back of a spoon.

Stand six 125 ml (4 fl oz/½ cup) ramekins in a large roasting tin and pour in water to a depth of 2.5 cm (1 inch). Divide the custard mixture equally between them. Bake in the oven for about 40 minutes, or until set.

Remove the ramekins from the water bath and allow to cool. Chill for at least 1 hour, or if possible overnight. Sprinkle the remaining sugar over the tops of the ramekins. Cook under a hot grill for 2-3 minutes to caramelize the sugar. Chill again for at least 2 hours before serving, accompanied by fresh fruits.

Serves 6

CHOCOLATE DIPPED FRUITS AND NUTS

INGREDIENTS

*about 700g (1½ lb/5 cups) fruits - a
selection of physalis, strawberries
and kumquats*
*225g (8 oz/1 cup) good quality plain
(dark) chocolate, broken into pieces*
85g (3 oz/½ cup) shelled brazil nuts

METHOD

Preparation time: 30 minutes

To prepare the physalis carefully tear each 'lantern' open, peeling back the papery casing in strips to reveal the fruit. Holding the berry in one hand give the outer strips a gentle twist at the base to hold in shape. Wipe all the fruits making sure they are clean and dry.

Melt the chocolate in a bowl set over a pan of simmering water. The bottom of the bowl should not touch the water. Stir until smooth. Lay out sheets of baking parchment on trays or on a flat surface where the chocolates can cool and set.

Dip the fruits and nuts, one at a time, in the chocolate to half coat them. Set aside on the baking parchment to cool and set. Serve on the same day, arranged on a serving platter or individual plates

NOTE:
You can use milk or white chocolate if you prefer, or a selection. Eat them on the same day as they are made.

Serves 6-8

SCENTED RICE PUDDING

INGREDIENTS

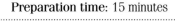

4 green cardamom pods
600 ml (1 pint/2 cups) milk
1 vanilla pod
85g (3 oz/⅓ cup) pudding rice
55g (2 oz/¼ cup) caster sugar
150 ml (¼ pint/⅔ cup) double
  (thick) cream
To decorate:
2 teaspoons grated pistachio nuts
few rose petals (optional)

METHOD   Preparation time: 15 minutes

Lightly crack the cardamom pods but do not remove the black seeds from the inside. Put the pods in a medium sized saucepan with the milk and vanilla pod. Bring to the boil.

Add the rice and sugar to the pan and bring back to boiling point. Lower the heat so the rice mixture is barely simmering, then cover and cook for 40-45 minutes until tender and creamy. Transfer to a bowl and leave to cool, covered closely with clingfilm to prevent a skin forming.

When the rice is cool remove the cardamom and vanilla pods. Whip the cream until it forms soft peaks and fold into the rice. Chill lightly before spooning into individual serving glasses. Serve sprinkled with grated pistachio and a few rose petals, if liked.

Serves 6

SCENTED RHUBARB FOOL

INGREDIENTS

450g (1 lb/4 cups) rhubarb, trimmed
85g (3 oz/⅓ cup) caster sugar
2 teaspoons orange flower water
250 ml (8 fl oz/1 cup) whipping
  cream
To decorate: mint sprigs

METHOD

Preparation time: 25–30 minutes

Wash the rhubarb and cut it into 2.5 cm (1 inch) lengths. Place in a saucepan with the caster sugar, cover and cook over a low heat for 15-20 minutes, until soft.

Purée the fruit in a processor or liquidizer or push through a sieve. Transfer to a large bowl and leave until cold. Stir in the orange flower water.

Whip the cream until it forms soft peaks. Fold into the cooled fruit. Spoon the fool into four individual serving glasses and chill slightly before serving, decorated with sprigs of mint.

NOTE:
For a lighter version replace some of the cream with fromage frais.

Serves 4

HONEY AND GINGER ICE CREAM

INGREDIENTS

*6 pieces stem ginger preserved in
  syrup*
*600 ml (1 pint/2 cups) whipping
  cream*
225g (8 oz/1 cup) clear honey
*To serve: brandy snap biscuits or
  chocolate thins*

METHOD   **Preparation time:** 20 minutes

Set freezer to rapid freeze. Rinse the ginger pieces and dry with kitchen paper. Cut into small pieces and then chop finely using a large cook's knife. Set aside.

In a large bowl, whip the cream until it forms soft peaks. Fold in the chopped ginger and the honey. Pour the mixture into a rigid container, cover and freeze for 1 hour or until slushy and ice particles have formed.

Remove the ice cream from the freezer and return to a clean bowl. Whisk until smooth. Return to the freezer container, cover and continue to freeze until solid. Remember to return freezer to normal setting. Serve the ice cream accompanied by brandy snap biscuits or chocolate thins.

Serves 6

MAPLE, WALNUT AND CHOCOLATE ICE CREAM

INGREDIENTS

*600 ml (1 pint/2 cups) whipping
  cream*
150 ml (¼ pint/⅔ cup) maple syrup
85g (3 oz/⅓ cup) walnuts, chopped
*85g (3 oz/⅓ cup) good quality plain
  (dark) chocolate*
To decorate: scented geranium leaves

METHOD

Preparation time: 25 minutes

Set freezer to rapid freeze. In a large bowl whip the cream until it forms soft peaks. Fold in the maple syrup and the walnuts. Transfer to a rigid freezer-proof container, cover and freeze for 2-3 hours until slushy.

Meanwhile, coarsely grate the chocolate on to a plate and chill in the fridge until required. (The chocolate can be chopped into small pieces using a large cooks knife if preferred).

Transfer the ice cream mixture to a clean bowl and stir well with a wooden spoon. Stir in the prepared chocolate and return to the rigid container, cover and freeze again until firm. Serve scoops of ice cream in individual serving dishes decorated with scented geranium leaves. Remember to return freezer to normal setting.

Serves 6

CRÈME CARAMELS

INGREDIENTS

Caramel:
115g (4 oz/½ cup) caster sugar
4 tablespoons water
Custard:
450 ml (¾ pint/1¾ cups) creamy
*   milk*
2 tablespoons caster sugar
2 eggs
½-1 teaspoon vanilla essence

METHOD

Preparation time: 25 minutes

Preheat the oven to 190° C/375°F/ Gas 5. Warm four dariole moulds in the oven. To make the caramel put the sugar and water in a small heavy based saucepan. Stir gently over a low heat until the sugar has completely dissolved. Increase the heat and boil, without stirring, until the syrup becomes a rich golden brown in colour. Do not overbrown.

Pour the caramel into the warmed dariole moulds, each to a depth of about 2 cm (¾ inch). Carefully tilt each mould to coat the sides with caramel. Stand the moulds in a roasting tin. Place the milk and sugar in a clean pan and heat until almost boiling. Meanwhile, beat the eggs together then pour the milk onto the eggs and beat well. Strain into a measuring jug. Stir in the vanilla essence then pour the custard into the prepared moulds. Fill the roasting tin with hot water to a depth of about 3.5 cm (1½ inches).

Cover the moulds with a sheet of baking parchment or foil. Bake in the oven for 40 minutes until lightly set then remove from the roasting tin and allow to cool. Chill for at least 1 hour. To unmould, invert the moulds onto individual serving plates or shallow bowls and lightly shake loose. Take care as the golden caramel will run and pool around the custards.

Serves 4

INGREDIENTS

4 ripe peaches
55g (2 oz/¼ cup) toasted flaked
almonds
300g (10 oz/1¼ cups) crème fraîche
about 1 teaspoon ground cinnamon
85g (3 oz/⅓ cup) soft light brown
sugar

METHOD   Preparation time: 15 minutes

Halve and stone the peaches and then slice into one large or four individual heat-proof serving dishes (large individual ramekins will do). Sprinkle the toasted almond flakes evenly over the peaches.

Spoon the crème fraîche over the peaches to thickly cover and spread evenly. Lightly sprinkle the crème fraîche with the ground cinnamon. Preheat the grill to hot. Sprinkle the sugar over the surface of the crème fraîche to completely cover and place under the hot grill for 3-4 minutes until caramelised. Cool and then chill for at least one hour before serving.

VARIATION:
You can vary the fruit to include strawberries, loganberries, raspberries, mango or papaya.

Serves 4

INGREDIENTS

Crumble topping:
150g (5 oz/²⁄₃ cup) plain flour
25g (1 oz/2 tablespoons) rolled oats
55g (2 oz/¹⁄₄ cup) ground almonds
85g (3 oz/¹⁄₃ cup) butter, plus extra
* for greasing*
55g (2 oz/¹⁄₄ cup) demerara sugar
700g (1¹⁄₂ lb/5 cups) fresh ripe
* apricots*
55g (2 oz/¹⁄₄ cup) caster sugar
2 tablespoons lemon juice
2 tablespoons chopped almonds
To serve: whipped cream or custard

METHOD

Preparation time: 20 minutes

Preheat the oven to 180° C/350° F/ Gas 4. Grease a baking dish with butter. To make the crumble topping, sieve the flour into a mixing bowl and stir in the rolled oats and ground almonds. Rub in the butter. Stir in the demerara sugar. Set aside.

Halve and stone the apricots. Cut into quarters if large. Place in the bottom of the prepared baking dish and sprinkle with the caster sugar and the lemon juice. Spoon over the crumble mixture to cover completely.

Sprinkle the chopped almonds over the crumble and bake in the preheated oven for about 35-40 minutes, until golden brown. Serve hot or warm with cream or custard.

Serves 4

SPICED APPLE PIE

INGREDIENTS

Sweet Shortcrust Pastry:
225g (8 oz/1 cup) plain white flour
pinch of salt
115g (4 oz/½ cup) butter, in pieces
25g (1 oz/2 tablespoons) caster
  sugar
1 egg yolk
2 teaspoons lemon juice
about 2 tablespoons iced water
Filling:
700g (1½ lb/6 cups) cooking apples,
  eg Bramleys
55g (2 oz/¼ cup) caster sugar, plus
  extra for dredging
¼ teaspoon ground cloves
1 teaspoon ground cinnamon
a little milk to glaze

METHOD

Preparation time: 30 minutes

Preheat the oven to 200° C/400°F/ Gas 6 15 mins before baking pie. Grease a 23-25 cm (9-10 inch) pie plate. Sift the flour and salt into a large bowl. Lightly rub in the butter then stir in the sugar. Make a well in the centre of the mixture and drop in the egg yolk. Add the lemon juice and a tablespoon of iced water. Mix to a dough using a palette knife, adding extra water as necessary. Turn on to a floured surface and knead lightly. Wrap and chill for 15-20 minutes.

Meanwhile, peel, core, halve and slice the apples. Place in a bowl and sprinkle with the sugar and spices. Toss to mix. Divide the pastry in two. On a lightly floured surface roll out half and use to line the prepared pie plate. Place the apple mixture over the pastry, piling it in the centre. Dampen the pastry edges with a little water. Roll out the remaining pastry and use to cover the pie. Press the edges to seal and trim away the excess pastry.

Use pastry trimmings to decorate the pie and make two or three small holes in the top to allow steam to escape. Brush pie with a little milk and sprinkle with caster sugar. Bake the pie in the oven for 20 minutes then lower the heat to 180° C/350°F/Gas 4 and continue baking for a further 15-20 minutes until the pastry is golden brown.
Serve the pie hot or warm with custard or lightly whipped cream.

Serves 6

STEAMED GOOSEBERRY AND ALMOND PUDDINGS

INGREDIENTS

175g (6 oz/1½ cup) gooseberries,
* fresh or frozen*
115g (4 oz/½ cup) shredded suet
115g (4 oz/½ cup) fresh white
* breadcrumbs*
115g (4 oz/½ cup) soft light brown
* sugar*
pinch of salt
2 eggs
1 teaspoon almond essence
about 150 ml (¼ pint/⅔ cup) milk
oil for greasing
To serve: custard or whipped cream
To decorate: gooseberry leaves

METHOD

Preparation time: 25 minutes

Top and tail the gooseberries if fresh, alternately allow to thaw if using frozen. Cut in half and place in a bowl with the suet, breadcrumbs, sugar and salt.

Beat together the eggs and almond essence. Stir into the dry ingredients, adding enough milk to give the mixture a soft dropping consistency. Leave to stand for 20 minutes.

Grease six 200 ml (7 fl oz/¾ cup) individual pudding basins and line the base of each with a small disc of baking parchment. Divide the pudding mixture between them and cover each tightly with oiled foil. Steam for 45 minutes-1 hour until firm. Leave to stand for 2 minutes, then turn out onto individual serving plates to serve. Serve with custard or whipped cream.

Serves 6

STEAMED CHOCOLATE PUDDING

INGREDIENTS

*55g (2 oz/¼ cup) good quality plain
(dark) chocolate*
115 ml (4 fl oz/½ cup) milk
*45g (1½ oz/2½ tablespoons) butter,
plus extra for greasing*
*45g (1½ oz/2½ tablespoons) caster
sugar*
2 eggs, separated
*115g (4 oz/½ cup) fresh white
breadcrumbs*
1 teaspoon baking powder, sifted
*To serve: single (light) cream and
chocolate sauce (see page 64)*

METHOD

Preparation time: 25 minutes

Butter the insides of 6 dariole moulds and line the base of each with a small disc of baking parchment. Grate the chocolate and place in a saucepan with the milk. Heat gently stirring until the chocolate has dissolved and is smooth. Allow to cool slightly.

In a large bowl, cream together the butter and sugar, until soft and fluffy. Beat in the egg yolks one at a time and then the cooled melted chocolate mixture, breadcrumbs and baking powder.

In a clean dry bowl, whisk the egg whites until fairly stiff and fold into the chocolate mixture. Spoon the mixture into the prepared moulds and cover each tightly with buttered foil. Steam for 30 minutes, or until firm. Leave to stand for 2 minutes, then turn out onto individual serving plates. Pour the cream around the pudding, dot the chocolate sauce on the cream and draw a cocktail stick through the sauce to feather the cream.

Serves 6

SPONGE FLAN WITH SPICED PLUMS

INGREDIENTS

Sponge flan:
2 eggs
45g (1½ oz/2½ tablespoons) caster
 sugar
55g (2 oz/¼ cup) plain flour
Spiced plums:
450g (1 lb/4 cups) plums
75g (3 oz/⅓ cup) caster sugar
¼ teaspoon ground cinnamon
300 ml (½ pint/1¼ cups) double
 (thick) cream
1 teaspoon demerara sugar
¼ teaspoon ground cinnamon

METHOD   Preparation time: 30 minutes

Preheat the oven to 200° C/400° F/ Gas 6. Grease a 20 cm (8 inch) sponge flan tin and line the centre with non-stick baking paper. In a large bowl set over a pan of hot water, whisk the eggs and sugar using an electric whisk until pale and thick enough to trail a ribbon of the mixture across the surface. Sift the flour and fold carefully into the egg mixture. Pour into the prepared tin and level the surface. Bake in the centre of the oven for about 20 minutes until well risen and golden. Turn out to cool on a wire rack.

Meanwhile to prepare the spiced plums, halve and stone them and put in a saucepan with the sugar and cinnamon. Cook over a gentle heat, stirring frequently for about 5 minutes until the plums are tender but not mushy. Using a slotted spoon transfer the plums to a bowl.

Continue cooking the juices for a few minutes until reduced and syrupy. Pour over the plums and leave until cold. To serve, whip the cream until it just holds its shape. Use half to fill the sponge flan case and arrange the spiced plums on top. Spoon the remaining cream around the top of the flan. Sprinkle the cream with the demerara sugar and cinnamon to finish.

Serves 6

INGREDIENTS

450g (1 lb/4 cups) semi-dried (no-soak) mixed fruit, eg apricots, prunes, figs, pears and apples
25g (1 oz/2 tablespoons) soft light brown sugar
300 ml (½ pint/1¼ cups) sweet dessert wine or orange juice
3 whole cloves
1 cinnamon stick, broken in two
grated zest of ½ orange
To decorate: thin strips of orange zest
To serve: crème fraîche or mascarpone cheese

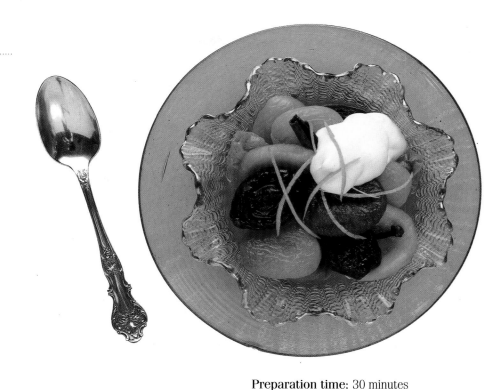

METHOD

Preparation time: 30 minutes

Put all the ingredients into a medium saucepan with 200 ml (7 fl oz/2/3 cup) water.

Bring to the boil, stirring, and then lower the heat, cover and simmer for 25 minutes until the fruit is plump.

Serve the fruit compôte hot in individual serving glasses, or chilled on plates decorated with strips of orange zest. Serve with scoops of crème fraîche or mascarpone cheese.

Serves 6

INGREDIENTS

8 small oranges
225g (8 oz/1 cup) granulated sugar
150ml (¼ pint/⅔ cup) water
4-6 tablespoons orange juice
To serve: crisp dessert biscuits

METHOD

Preparation time: 25 minutes

Pare the rind from 1 orange and shred finely. Simmer the rind in boiling water for 2 minutes then drain, refresh in cold water, drain then set aside. Using a small sharp knife, peel all the oranges, removing the white pith. Cut the flesh into thin slices and then using wooden cocktail sticks to secure, reassemble each orange. Arrange in a serving dish or individual dishes.

Put the sugar and water into a saucepan. Heat gently, stirring, until the sugar has completely dissolved and then bring to the boil and boil rapidly until a rich brown caramel is formed. Remove from the heat.

Carefully add enough orange juice to the caramel to give a syrupy coating consistency. Return to the heat and stir lightly to blend. Add the reserved orange rind. Pour the caramel sauce over the oranges and chill for at least 2 hours before serving, with crisp dessert biscuits.

Serves 4

PEARS IN SPICED WINE

INGREDIENTS

6 even-sized dessert pears
200g (7 oz/1 cup) granulated sugar
150 ml (¼ pint/⅔ cup) water
300 ml (½ pint/1¼ cups) red wine
strip of orange peel
4 cloves
2 small cinnamon sticks (or 1 large)
To serve: double (thick) cream

METHOD

Preparation time: 20 minutes

To choose the right sized saucepan for cooking, stand the pears upright in a pan just large enough to hold them all. Leave pears while preparing the syrup. Put the sugar and water into the pan. Cook, stirring, on a gentle heat until the sugar has dissolved. Bring to the boil and boil for 2 minutes.

Using a potato peeler, peel the pears but do not remove the stalks and cores. Stand them in the pan of syrup. Pour the red wine over the pears and add the orange peel, cloves and cinnamon sticks, broken in two. Poach the pears on a gentle heat for 25-35 minutes until tender. The exact time will depend on the ripeness of the pears and their size.

Using a slotted spoon, carefully lift out the pears and transfer them to a bowl. Bring the red wine syrup back to boiling point and boil rapidly until reduced by half. Strain over the pears and leave until cooled, rotating them in the syrup occasionally. Chill the pears for at least one hour before serving, turning them in the syrup from time to time. Serve one pear per person standing in a pool of syrup on individual serving plates. Accompany with double (thick) cream.

Serves 6

CHOCOLATE POTS

INGREDIENTS

*175g (6 oz/³/₄ cup) good quality plain
   (dark) chocolate*
*300 ml (¹/₂ pint/1¹/₄ cups) double
   (thick) cream*
small pinch of salt
2 tablespoons brandy or liqueur
*To decorate: 6 tablespoons double
   (thick) cream*
cocoa powder, to dust

METHOD

Preparation time: 10 minutes

Chop the chocolate into small pieces.
Put the cream and salt in a medium
saucepan. Heat until it reaches
boiling point and add the chocolate.
Using a wire whisk beat until smooth.
Stir in the brandy or liqueur.

Divide the mixture between four
chocolate mousse pots or small
ramekins smooth the top then leave
to cool. Chill in fridge until set (at
least 2 hours).

Just before serving, whip the cream
until it stands in soft peaks. Spoon on
to each chocolate pot and top with a
fine dusting of cocoa powder.

NOTE:
Use a chocolate with a high
percentage of cocoa solids - the
better the chocolate, the better the
result.

Serves 4

– 4 –
GRAND PUDDINGS

WHITE CHOCOLATE MOUSSE WITH CHOCOLATE SAUCE

INGREDIENTS
....

Chocolate sauce:
115g (4 oz/½ cup) plain (dark)
  chocolate
25g (1 oz/2 tablespoons) butter
3 tablespoons water
3 tablespoons brandy
White chocolate mousse:
225g (8 oz/1 cup) white chocolate,
  broken into pieces
55g (2 oz/¼ cup) unsalted butter, at
  room temperature
3 egg yolks
300 ml (½ pint/1¼ cups) double
  (thick) cream
2 tablespoons caster sugar
To decorate: shavings of white
  chocolate and cocoa powder

METHOD
....

Preparation time: 30 minutes
....

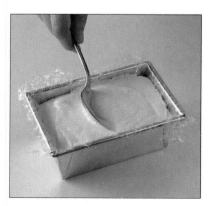

To make the dark chocolate sauce, put the chocolate, butter and water in a small saucepan. Heat, stirring constantly, over a gentle heat until smooth and melted. Stir in the brandy and leave to cool.

Line a 750 ml (1½ pint/3 cup) loaf tin with clingfilm. Melt the white chocolate in a large bowl over a pan of hot, not boiling water. Remove from the heat. Add the butter in pieces and beat until well mixed. Stir in the egg yolks.

Whip the cream with the sugar until it just holds its shape and fold into the chocolate mixture. Spoon the mixture into the prepared tin. Tap the tin on the work surface to settle and level the mixture. Cover and chill for at least 4 hours, or overnight, until firm.

To serve whole, turn the mousse out onto a flat serving plate and peel off the cling film. Lightly smooth the surfaces of the mousse with a palette knife.

Cover the top with large shavings of white chocolate and dredge with a little cocoa powder. Serve accompanied with the dark chocolate sauce.

For individual servings, turn the mousse out onto a board and smooth the surface as above. Cut into slices and arrange on individual serving plates with a pool of sauce and some shavings of white chocolate, lightly dusted with cocoa.

Serves 6

Left: if you want an alternative to Chocolate Sauce, try serving the mousse with Coffee Sauce (see page 72)

STRAWBERRY BOATS

INGREDIENTS

*225g (8 oz/1 cup) sweet shortcrust
  pastry (see page 55)*
3 tablespoons strawberry conserve
*175g (6 oz/³⁄₄ cup) cream cheese,
  softened*
1 tablespoon caster or vanilla sugar
2 tablespoons single (light) cream
12 fairly large strawberries
*4 tablespoons redcurrant jelly
double (thick) cream*
To decorate: strawberry leaves

METHOD

Preparation time: 30 minutes

Preheat the oven to 200° C/400° F/
Gas 6. Grease 12 boat shaped tartlet
tins. On a lightly floured surface roll
out the pastry and use to line the
tartlet tins. Prick the bases with a
fork and chill for 15 minutes. Bake in
the oven for 10-15 minutes until pale
golden.

Spoon a little strawberry conserve on
the base of each tartlet while they are
still warm then leave to cool. In a
small bowl mix together the cream
cheese, sugar and cream until
smooth. Divide between the tartlets
and smooth the surface level with a
teaspoon.

Thickly slice each strawberry and
arrange one on each tartlet. Melt the
redcurrant jelly in a small pan on a
gentle heat. Use a brush to paint the
jelly over the strawberries. Leave to
set. To serve, pool a little double
(thick) cream on individual serving
plates and place two strawberry
boats on each. Decorate with
strawberry leaves.

Serves 6

INDIVIDUAL HAZELNUT MERINGUES

INGREDIENTS

Meringues:
55g (2 oz/¼ cup) shelled hazelnuts
2 egg whites
115g (4 oz/½ cup) soft light brown
sugar
350g (12 oz/1½ cups) raspberries
225g (8 oz/1 cup) crème fraîche or
double (thick) cream
To decorate: raspberry leaves or
lemon balm

METHOD

Preparation time: 25 minutes

Preheat the oven to 120° C/250° F/ Gas ½. Line two oiled baking sheets with non-stick baking parchment. Draw six 7.5 cm (3 inch) circles and six 5 cm (2 inch) circles on the paper Using a food processor or blender, grind the hazelnuts quite finely. In a large bowl whisk the egg whites until stiff. Add half of the sugar and whisk again. Add the remaining sugar a little at a time, whisking after each addition. Fold in the ground hazelnuts.

Put the meringue into a piping bag fitted with a large plain nozzle. Pipe on to the baking parchment circles to cover completely. Bake in the oven for about 1½ hours or until crisp. Remove from the baking parchment and cool on wire racks. Just before serving, assemble the meringues. Set aside half of the raspberries. Using a fork, lightly mash the rest in a shallow bowl.

Spoon three-quarters of the crème fraîche or lightly whipped double (thick) cream on to the larger meringue circles and divide the mashed raspberries between them. Cover with the small meringues and spoon the remaining crème fraîche or cream on top. Place on a serving platter or individual serving plates and scatter the remaining raspberries over and around. Serve decorated with raspberry leaves or lemon balm.

Serves 6

CHOCOLATE BRANDY ROULADE

INGREDIENTS

4 eggs
175g (6 oz/³/₄ cup) caster sugar
55g (2 oz/¹/₄ cup) cocoa powder,
  sifted
2 egg whites
icing sugar, for sifting
300ml (¹/₂ pint/1¹/₄ cups) double
  (thick) cream
4 tablespoons brandy
85g (3 oz/¹/₃ cup) good quality plain
  (dark) chocolate, grated
extra cocoa powder, for sifting
To decorate: chocolate thins or
  chocolate rose leaves

METHOD   **Preparation time:** 30 minutes

Preheat the oven to 200° C/400° F/ Gas 6. Lightly oil a Swiss roll tin and line with non-stick baking parchment. In a large bowl set over a pan of simmering water, whisk the whole eggs and sugar until pale and thick. Remove from the heat. Using a large metal spoon, gently fold in the cocoa powder.

In a clean bowl whisk the egg whites until stiff. Fold into the cocoa mixture. Pour the mixture into the prepared tin and level the surface. Bake in the oven for 15 minutes or until set. While the roulade is cooking, have ready a clean damp tea cloth. Sprinkle a sheet of non-stick baking parchment with sifted icing sugar.

When the roulade is cooked, remove from the oven and leave to stand for 2 minutes. Cover with the damp tea cloth and leave for a further 10 minutes. Turn the roulade out onto the dusted baking parchment and peel away the paper from the roulade. Cover again with the damp cloth and leave until completely cooled.

To finish the roulade, whip the cream and brandy together until soft peaks form. Sprinkle the grated chocolate over the roulade and trim away the edges. Spread the cream over. Using the paper to help, roll up the cake like a Swiss roll. It might crack a little. Dust with cocoa powder.

Serve the roulade in slices on individual plates dusted with a little cocoa powder and icing sugar. Decorate with chocolate thins, cut into triangles, or chocolate rose leaves if time allows.

Serves 6

VARIATION:
Chocolate and Raspberry Roulade
When filling the roulade, omit the brandy and grated chocolate. Lightly mash 115g (4 oz/¾ cup) raspberries with a fork. Sprinkle over the roulade then cover with whipped cream and roll up as before. Dredge with cocoa powder and decorate with raspberries.

CHOCOLATE ROSE LEAVES

Rose leaves
85g (3 oz/⅓ cup) good quality plain (dark) chocolate, in pieces (at least 50% cocoa solids)

Wash the rose leaves and dry them thoroughly. Melt the chocolate in a bowl set over a pan of simmering water. The water should not touch the bottom of the bowl. Remove the bowl from the pan. Using a fairly small brush, paint the underside of each rose leaf with melted chocolate. Leave on non-stick baking parchment in a cool, dry place to set and then carefully peel each leaf away from the chocolate.

Left: a selection of chocolate rose leaves

INGREDIENTS

200g (7 oz/³⁄₄ cup) unsalted butter, softened, plus extra for greasing
200g (7 oz/³⁄₄ cup) (dark) plain chocolate
4 eggs, separated
200g (7 oz/1 cup) caster sugar
To serve
softly whipped double (thick) cream
cocoa powder, for dusting 225g (8 oz/2 cups) fraises des bois (alpine strawberries) or blueberries

---

METHOD   **Preparation time:** 15-20 minutes

Preheat the oven to 190° F/375° F/ Gas 5. Grease a 20 cm (8 inch) springform cake tin with butter and line the base with non-stick baking parchment. Chop the chocolate into small pieces and melt in a large bowl set over a pan of simmering water. (The water should not touch the base of the bowl). Add the butter and stir until smooth. Remove from the heat and set aside.

Put the egg yolks and half of the sugar into another bowl. Whisk until pale and thick. Add the chocolate mixture and whisk lightly together until blended. In a clean bowl whisk the egg whites until stiff. Add the remaining sugar and whisk again. Using a large metal spoon fold into the chocolate mixture. Pour the mixture into the prepared tin and bake for 40 minutes, or until the centre is just firm. Remove from the oven and leave to cool in the tin for at least 15 minutes before turning out. Serve warm or cold.

To serve, cut the cake into slices. Serve each slice on large individual plates with a spoonful of softly whipped cream on the side. Dust the cream and plate with a little cocoa powder and scatter over a few fraises des bois or blueberries.

NOTE:
This is a flourless cake with a heavenly, rich soft texture. Don't worry if the surface cracks a little – that is as it should be.

Serves 6

MILLE FEUILLES

INGREDIENTS

*450g (1 lb/2 cups) frozen puff
  pastry, defrosted*
4 tablespoons strawberry conserve
*2 tablespoons Grand Marnier or
  Cointreau*
*300 ml (½ pint/1¾ cups) double
  (thick) cream*
*3 tablespoons icing sugar, plus extra
  for dusting*
To serve: fresh strawberries
To decorate: strawberry leaves

METHOD

Preparation time: 25 minutes

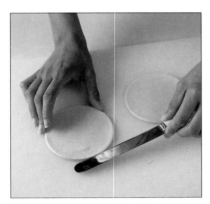

Preheat the oven to 230° C/450° F/
Gas 8. Lightly oil a large baking sheet.
On a lightly floured surface, roll out
the pastry to 6mm (¼ inch) thickness.
Using a 8.5 cm (3½ inch) plain metal
cutter, cut out six rounds. Use a
round-bladed knife to knock up the
pastry edges. This will help the pastry
to rise. Place the rounds on the
prepared baking sheet and prick over
the surface lightly with a fork. Chill
for 20 minutes.

Bake the pastry rounds in the oven
for 10-15 minutes until well risen and
golden. Transfer to a wire rack to
cool, then split each in half to give 12
pastry rounds. In a small bowl or cup
stir together the strawberry conserve
and liqueur. In a separate bowl whip
the cream and 3 tablespoons icing
sugar until soft peaks form. On four
individual serving plates layer three
pastry rounds, sandwiching them
with the flavoured conserve and
cream. Finish with a pastry layer.

Liberally dredge the top of each mille
feuille with icing sugar. Over a gas
flame or electric ring heat a long
metal skewer until red hot. Carefully
holding the skewer, using an oven
glove or cloth, sear a lattice pattern
into the sugar, reheating the skewer
as necessary. Serve the mille feuilles
with the strawberries, decorated with
strawberry leaves.

Serves 4

CHOCOLATE BAVAROIS WITH COFFEE SAUCE

INGREDIENTS

4 egg yolks
55g (2 oz/¼ cup) caster sugar
150 ml (¼ pint/⅔ cup) single (light) cream
115g (4 oz/½ cup) plain (dark) chocolate, grated
1 teaspoon vanilla essence
2 teaspoons powdered gelatine
300 ml (½ pint/1¾ cups) double (thick) cream
Coffee sauce:
300 ml (½ pint/1¾ cups) very strong black coffee
55g (2 oz/¼ cup) caster sugar
1 tablespoon cornflour
4 tablespoons double (thick) cream
2 tablespoons brandy
To decorate: 3 tablespoons double (thick) cream

METHOD

Preparation time: 30 minutes

Lightly oil six individual pudding basins or small moulds. In a large heat-proof bowl whisk together the egg yolks and sugar until pale and thick. Put the single (light) cream and chocolate into a pan. Heat until almost boiling then pour over the egg mixture, stirring constantly.

Place the bowl over a pan of simmering water and heat, stirring, until the mixture thickens. Strain into a clean bowl and stir in the vanilla essence. Put three tablespoons of cold water into a small bowl or cup. Sprinkle over the gelatine and leave until spongy. Stand in a pan of hot water and stir until the gelatine has dissolved.

Stir into the chocolate custard and leave to cool slightly, stirring frequently to prevent a skin forming. Do not allow to set. Whip 300 ml (½ pint/1¾ cups) of double (thick) cream until it forms soft peaks. Fold into the chocolate custard and pour the mixture into the prepared moulds. Chill for 1 hour, until set.

Meanwhile, make the coffee sauce: put the coffee and sugar in a pan and heat gently, stirring until the sugar has dissolved. Slake the cornflour with 2 tablespoons cold water, then stir into the coffee.

Simmer, stirring, for 1 minute then transfer to a bowl or jug. Leave until cold, stirring occasionally to prevent a skin forming. Lightly whip the cream and fold into the sauce with the brandy.

Pool the coffee sauce on to six serving plates. Dip the moulds into warm water for a few seconds, turn out on to the sauce.Dot the remaining cream on the sauce round each bavarois and draw a cocktail stick through each dot to feather the cream.

Serves 6

CREME ANGLAISE

1 teaspoon vanilla essence
300 ml (¹/₂ pint/1³/₄ cups) milk
3 egg yolks
25g (1oz/2 tablespoons) caster
* sugar*
6 tablespoons double (thick)
cream, lightly whipped

Put the egg yolks and sugar in a bowl and add the vanilla essence. Heat the milk to just below boiling. Whisk the egg yolks and sugar until thick and light, then whisk in the hot milk. Return the mixture to the pan (or to a double boiler) and cook over a very low heat, stirring constantly, until it thickens slightly. It should just coat the back of a wooden spoon. Do not boil or the custard will curdle. Strain the custard into a clean bowl and leave until completely cooled. Fold in the lightly whipped cream and chill for at least 30 minutes before serving.

Right: here the Chocolate Bavarois is served with Crème Anglaise sauce, and garnished with a scented geranium leaf.

INGREDIENTS

*175g (6 oz/1½ cups) redcurrants,
 stalks removed*
*175g (6 oz/1½ cups) blackcurrants,
 stalks removed*
*6 tablespoons sweet white wine or
 water*
100g (3½ oz/½ cup) caster sugar
2 eggs
1 egg yolk
3 teaspoons powdered gelatine
*300 ml (½ pint/1¼ cups) double
 (thick) cream*
To decorate:
*300 ml (½ pint/1¼ cups) double
 (thick) or whipping cream*
about 32 langues de chat biscuits
*fresh stalks of red and blackcurrants
 with leaves, if available*

METHOD

Preparation time: 30 minutes

Put the red and blackcurrants in a pan with 3 tablespoons of the sweet wine or water and 2 tablespoons of the sugar. Cook on a medium heat, stirring frequently, for 7-8 minutes until the fruit has softened.

Cool slightly then purée in a blender or food processor. Finally, push the fruit through a sieve and set aside. Lightly oil an 18cm (7 inch) deep cake tin or soufflé dish.

Put the remaining sugar, eggs and egg yolk into a large bowl and whisk until pale and very thick. In a small bowl or cup dissolve the gelatine in the remaining sweet wine or water. Whip 300 ml (½ pint/1¼ cups) of cream until it stands in soft peaks.

Using a large metal spoon, fold the currant purée into the egg mixture and fold in the dissolved gelatine. Carefully fold in the cream. Pour the mixture into the prepared cake tin or soufflé dish and chill until set (at least 1 hour).

To unmould and serve the charlotte, dip the cake tin or soufflé dish in warm water for a few seconds, and invert on to a serving plate. Shake loose and carefully lift away the tin. Whip the remaining cream until it stands in soft peaks. Spread about one-third around the sides of the charlotte.

Arrange the langues de chat, slightly overlapping, around the edge of the charlotte, pressing them into the cream. Spoon the remaining cream around the top of the charlotte and decorate with stalks of fresh red and blackcurrants, with leaves if available.

Serves 8

GELATINE

To ensure perfect results with gelatine, sprinkle it lightly over the surface of the cold liquid in a small bowl or cup. Leave to stand for a few moments until the gelatine absorbs the liquid and it appears 'spongy'. Stand the bowl or cup in a pan of gently simmering water and stir the gelatine mixture until dissolved.

If the mixture to be set is very cold, add a little to the dissolved gelatine to 'lighten' before stirring in. Otherwise add the dissolved gelatine in a thin stream, stirring constantly.

Gelatine is an animal product and unsuitable for vegetarians. An alternative, Agar Agar, is available from health shops.

Left: Fresh Currant Charlotte is an easy but impressive dessert for any dinner party.

INGREDIENTS

55g (2 oz/¼ cup) fresh root ginger, grated
100g (3½ oz/½ cup) demerara sugar
55g (2 oz/¼ cup) granulated sugar
300 ml (½ pint/1¼ cups) water
2 ripe nectarines
1 charentais melon or other orange fleshed melon
12 physalis
225g (8 oz/1 cup) crème fraîche

METHOD   **Preparation time:** 30 minutes

Peel and coarsely grate the ginger. Place in a saucepan with the sugars and pound them together using a wooden spoon to release the flavour. Add the water and heat until boiling. Lower the heat and allow to simmer uncovered for about 20 minutes, stirring frequently, until reduced and syrupy. There should be a little less than half the original amount.

Sieve the ginger syrup into a clean bowl, pressing the ginger pulp with a wooden spoon to release as much of the flavour as possible. Allow to cool and chill if time allows. To serve, halve and stone the nectarines and cut the flesh into thin slices. Halve the melon and remove the seeds. Scoop the flesh from the inside and cut into bite-sized pieces. Remove the physalis berries from their papery lanterns and cut each in half.

Arrange the fruit on serving plates and place a spoonful of crème fraîche on one side of each. Spoon the prepared ginger syrup over the fruit and crème fraîche. Serve at once.

Serves 4-6

FRUIT PAVLOVA

INGREDIENTS

3 egg whites
pinch of salt
175g (6 oz/ ¾ cup) caster sugar
1 teaspoon cornflour
1 teaspoon white vinegar
300 ml (½ pint/1¼ cups) double
* (thick) cream*
1 ripe peach or nectarine
1 small star fruit
115g (4 oz/½ cup) raspberries
2 passionfruits

METHOD

Preparation time: 20 minutes

Preheat the oven to 150° C/300° F/ Gas 2. Oil a large baking sheet and line with baking parchment. Draw a 22.5 cm (9 inch) circle on the parchment. Put the egg whites and salt into a large bowl and whisk until stiff. Whisk in half of the sugar.

Mix together the cornflour and the remaining sugar. Fold into the meringue using a large metal spoon. Finally fold in the vinegar. Spoon the meringue on to the prepared baking sheet, spreading to fill the marked circle. Use the back of a spoon to create a shallow hollow in the centre. Bake in the oven for 1 hour, then remove to a wire rack, still on the paper, to cool. Remove the paper when cold.

To serve, whip the cream until it just holds its shape. Spread over the meringue. Stone and thinly slice the peach or nectarine and slice the star fruit. Arrange on the pavlova with the raspberries. Halve the passionfruits and spoon the seeds over the cream and fruit and then serve.

NOTE:
A good pavlova should be crisp on the outside and soft and melting within. Vary the fruit according to personal taste or availability.

Serves 6-8

MERINGUE AND FRUIT PYRAMID

INGREDIENTS

Meringues:
3 egg whites
175g (6 oz/³/₄ cup) caster sugar
Filling:
450ml (³/₄ pint/2 cups) double (thick)
  or whipping cream
icing sugar, for dusting
450g (1 lb/4 cups) mixed summer
  fruits eg raspberries, red and white
  currants, strawberries, blueberries
rose petals or other edible flowers
  (optional)
To serve: extra pouring cream, or
  Chocolate Sauce (see page 64)
  or Mango Sauce (see page 14)

METHOD   **Preparation time:** 20-25 minutes

Preheat the oven to 110° C/225° F/ Gas ¼. Lightly oil two baking sheets and line with non-stick baking parchment or lightly oiled greaseproof paper.

Put the egg whites in a large bowl and whisk until stiff and dry. Add half of the sugar and whisk in. Using a large metal spoon fold in the remaining sugar.

Using a 1 cm (½ inch) plain nozzle, pipe the meringue mixture into mounds on the prepared baking sheets. You should get about 24 mounds. Bake in the oven for 2-2½ hours until crisp. You can store the cooled meringues in an airtight tin until required.

To assemble the dessert, whip the cream until it holds its shape. Reserve about one third and use the remainder to sandwich the meringues in pairs.

Spread a little of the reserved cream in the centre of a large serving platter. Arrange the meringues as a pyramid on the plate using the rest of the cream to help secure the structure. Dust with a little icing sugar.

Arrange the fruits among and around the meringues and decorate with the rose petals and other edible flowers, if liked. Serve accompanied by a little extra pouring cream or Chocolate or Mango Sauce.

Serves 6

EXOTIC MERINGUE AND FRUIT PYRAMID

When summer fruits are either not available or not at their best, try using exotic fruits which are always in season. Arrange sliced mango or papaya and passion fruit halves around the base of the pyramid and tuck physalis among the meringues.

Right: This is a stunning dessert which takes little time to prepare. The meringues need slow drying in the oven but this can be done in advance and the dessert assembled at the last minute. It makes a lovely alternative wedding or special occasion cake.

VANILLA SPONGE WITH STRAWBERRIES AND CREAM

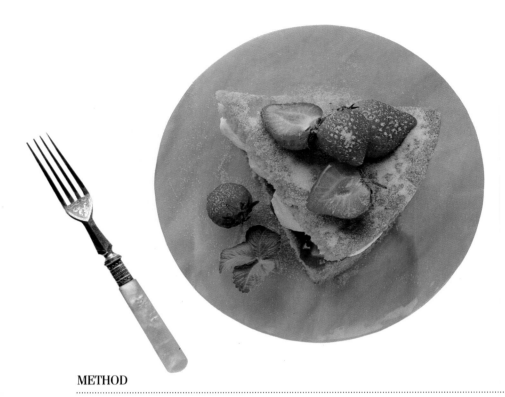

INGREDIENTS

115g (4 oz/½ cup) caster sugar, plus
   extra for dusting
115g (4 oz/1 cup) plain flour, plus
   extra for dusting
4 eggs
½ teaspoon vanilla essence
3 tablespoons Framboise liqueur,
   Cointreau or Grand Marnier
200 ml (7 fl oz/ ¾ cup) double (thick)
   cream
450g (1 lb/3 cups) strawberries
3 tablespoons strawberry conserve
icing sugar, for dusting
vanilla sugar or caster sugar, for
   dusting
To decorate: strawberry leaves

METHOD   **Preparation time:** 30 minutes

Preheat the oven to 190° C/375° F/
Gas 5. Lightly oil two 20 cm (8 inch)
sandwich tins and line the bases with
non-stick baking parchment. Mix
together 2 teaspoons each of sugar
and flour and use to dust the insides
of the cake tins. Tip out the excess.

In a large bowl set over a pan of
simmering water whisk together eggs,
vanilla essence and caster sugar until
very pale and thick. A 'trail' of
mixture should hold its shape on the
surface for several seconds before
sinking.

Sift half the flour into the egg mixture
and fold in using a large metal spoon.
Repeat, using remaining flour. Divide
the mixture between the two
prepared tins, tilting them to spread
evenly. Place both cakes on the
centre shelf in the preheated oven for
25 minutes or until the cakes are well
risen and beginning to shrink from the
sides of the tins.

Allow to cool in the tins slightly before turning out on to a wire rack. Remove lining paper from the bases of the cakes and sprinkle the cakes with the liqueur of your choice. Leave to cool completely. Whip the cream until it stands in soft peaks. Chop about 75g (3 oz/½ cup) of the strawberries.

Transfer one of the cakes, base upwards, on to a large serving plate. Stir the strawberry conserve to soften and use to spread over the surface. Sprinkle over the chopped strawberries and spoon the cream on top. Carefully place the second cake on top. Dust lightly with icing sugar.

Arrange the remaining strawberries on top and around the sponge in a casual tumbling manner. Decorate with strawberry leaves if available. Dust the fruit with vanilla or caster sugar to finish.

Serves 6-8

VARIATION

Substitute the strawberries for 2 ripe peaches. Chop the flesh of half and arrange the rest thinly sliced on top of the sponge. Use peach or apricot conserve in place of strawberry, and replace the Framboise with brandy or peach brandy, Cointreau or Grand Marnier. Decorate with mint sprigs.

Left: fresh fruit with flowers make this a beautiful summer dessert.

CHOCOLATE AND VANILLA ICE CREAM GÂTEAU

INGREDIENTS

....

1 litre (1 qt) good quality chocolate ice cream

1 litre (1 qt) good quality vanilla ice cream

300ml (½ pint/1¾ cups) double (thick) cream

cocoa powder, for dusting

chocolate curls (see page 84)

To serve: tuilles or other crisp dessert biscuits, frosted fruit and leaves

METHOD   Preparation time: 15 minutes

Set freezer to rapid freeze. Line the base of a loose bottomed 15 cm (6 inch) deep cake tin with non-stick baking parchment or lightly oiled greaseproof paper. Spoon half of the chocolate ice cream into the base and using the back of a metal spoon, smooth out to cover the base. Freeze for at least 15 minutes. Cover with half of the vanilla ice cream and freeze again.

Repeat layering the remaining chocolate and vanilla ice cream to give four layers, freezing between each layer. Freeze the gâteau for at least 2 hours before turning out. Remember to return freezer to normal setting.

To serve: whip the cream until it stands in soft peaks. Invert the gâteau on to a large serving plate and remove the cake tin and lining paper. Place the cream in peaks around the top of the gâteau and dust the peaks with cocoa powder. Decorate the top with chocolate curls. Arrange frosted fruits and leaves around the gâteau with more chocolate curls, if liked. Serve with tuilles, or other crisp dessert biscuits.

Frosted fruits, leaves and flowers should be used the same day as they are made.

You will need:

1 egg white (or more for larger quantities) fruits, leaves and flowers for decoration, caster sugar

Make sure all fruit, leaves and flowers are clean and dry. Lightly beat the egg white until just frothy. Thickly dust caster sugar on to a small plate or saucer and have more sugar to hand.

Use a soft paintbrush to coat the fruits etc. with the egg white. Transfer to the plate of caster sugar and thickly dredge with sugar to coat. Gently shake off the excess. Transfer to a wire rack covered with greaseproof paper and leave to dry.

Serves 8

FROSTED FRUIT, LEAVES AND FLOWERS

Fresh fruits, leaves and blossoms covered with a glistening coat of fine sugar make beautiful decorations for many puddings, especially those chilled and iced.

Fruits suitable are clusters of grapes, strawberries, physalis and cherries. Also fresh currants, raspberries and blackberries when available, on the stem. Small fruit leaves of all kinds work well too.

For frosted flowers, whole flower heads or individual petals can be prepared. Suitable flowers are roses, sweet peas, freesias, primrose, geraniums and violets. Suitable leaves include mint, scented geranium and lemon balm.

Left: a selection of frosted fruit and flowers, which can be used to complement many desserts.

CHESTNUT MOUSSE

INGREDIENTS

*115g (4 oz/ ½ cup) plain (dark)
  chocolate*
*1 x 225g (8 oz/1 cup) can sweetened
  chestnut purée*
3 tablespoons brandy
*200 ml (7 fl oz/ ¾ cup) double (thick)
  cream*
plain (dark) chocolate curls
4 marrons glacés

METHOD

Preparation time: 20 minutes

Break the chocolate into pieces. Melt in a bowl set over a pan of simmering water. (The bottom of the bowl should not touch the water). Remove from the heat, stir until smooth and leave to cool slightly. Meanwhile in a fairly large bowl beat together the chestnut purée and brandy until well blended. In a separate bowl whip the cream until stiff.

Stir the melted chocolate into the chestnut mixture and then fold in the whipped cream. Spoon the mixture into four stemmed serving glasses and chill lightly before serving decorated with chocolate curls, handing a whole marron glacé with each.

CHOCOLATE CURLS
Impressive chocolate curls can be made using a sharp straight edged knife (i.e. not serrated). Shave curls from the back of a chocolate bar that is at room temperature. White chocolate works just as well.

Serves 4

– 5 –
TARTS AND TARTLETS

BAKED CURD TART WITH FRESH FRUITS

INGREDIENTS

For the biscuit base:
85g (3 oz/⅓ cup) butter
175g (6 oz/¾ cup) digestive biscuits,
  crushed
For the filling:
85g (3 oz/⅓ cup) butter
115g (4 oz/½ cup) caster sugar
finely grated rind and juice of 1 large
  lemon
450g (1 lb/2 cups) curd cheese
2 large eggs (size 1), separated
55g (2 oz/¼ cup) ground almonds
25g (1 oz/2 tablespoons) semolina
To serve: icing sugar, for dusting
  fresh summer fruits

METHOD

Preparation time: 25 minutes

Preheat the oven to 180° C/350° F/ Gas 4. Oil a deep 20 cm (8 inch) loose-bottomed or spring-formed cake tin and line the base with baking parchment or lightly oiled greaseproof paper. To make the biscuit base melt 85g (3 oz/⅓ cup) of butter in a saucepan. Stir in the crushed biscuits, mixing well. Press firmly into the base of the prepared tin. Bake in the preheated oven for 10 minutes.

Meanwhile, in a large bowl cream together the butter, sugar and lemon rind until light and fluffy. Gradually beat in the curd cheese, egg yolks and lemon juice. Fold in the ground almonds and semolina.

Whisk the egg whites until stiff and carefully fold into the cheese mixture. Pour into the tin and bake in the oven for 1 hour. Turn the oven off and leave the curd tart in the oven until cooled. Remove from the tin and chill before serving. Serve dusted with icing sugar and accompanied by fresh summer fruits.

Serves 8

PECAN TART

INGREDIENTS

*350g (12 oz/1½ cups) bought
  shortcrust pastry*
Filling:
175g (6 oz/1½ cups) pecan halves
115g (4 oz/½ cup) unsalted butter
*115g (4 oz/½ cup) soft light brown
  sugar*
3 tablespoons double (thick) cream
25g (1 oz/2 tablespoons) flour, sifted
*To serve: lightly whipped cream or
  ice cream*

METHOD

Preparation time: 25 minutes

Preheat the oven to 200° C/400° F/
Gas 6. Grease a 23 cm (9 inch) flan
ring or loose-bottomed tart tin. On a
lightly floured surface roll out the
pastry and use to line the prepared
ring or tin. Prick the base and chill for
at least 15 minutes. Line the tart shell
with kitchen or greaseproof paper and
fill with baking beans. Bake blind in
the oven for 10 minutes. Remove the
paper and beans and return to the
oven for a further 5 minutes to cook
the base. Lower the oven
temperature to 190° C/375° F/Gas 5.

Meanwhile, prepare the filling: set
aside 55g (2 oz/½ cup) of the pecan
halves and roughly chop the rest. In a
saucepan over a moderate heat melt
the butter and the sugar, stirring
constantly. Bring to the boil. Remove
from the heat and beat in the cream
and flour. Stir in the chopped nuts,
return to the heat and bring back to
the boil.

Spoon the filling into the prepared
tart shell and arrange the reserved
pecan halves on top. Bake in the oven
for 20-25 minutes until firm. Serve
cool but not chilled, with lightly
whipped cream or ice cream.

Serves 6-8

INGREDIENTS

1 quantity Sweet Shortcrust Pastry
(see page 55)
or 350g (12 oz/1½ cups) bought
sweet shortcrust pastry
4 tablespoons cornflour
300 ml (½ pint/1¼ cups) water
juice and finely grated zest of 3
lemons
115g (4 oz/½ cup) caster sugar
55g (2 oz/¼ cup) butter
3 egg yolks
Meringue topping:
3 egg whites
pinch of salt
175g (6 oz/¾ cup) caster sugar

METHOD

Preparation time: 30 minutes

Preheat the oven to 200° C/400° F/
Gas 6. Oil a deep 23 cm (9 inch)
loose-bottomed flan tin. On a lightly
floured surface roll out the pastry and
use to line the prepared tin. Prick the
base with a fork and chill for at least
15 minutes. Line the flan case with
kitchen or greaseproof paper and fill
with baking beans. Bake blind in the
oven for 10 minutes, then remove the
paper and baking beans and return to
the oven for a further 5 minutes to
cook the base. Reduce the oven
temperature to 180° C/350° F/Gas 4.

In a small bowl, mix the cornflour to a
paste with a little of the water. Put
the rest of the water in a saucepan
with the lemon juice and caster
sugar. Bring to the boil. Pour in the
cornflour mixture, stirring constantly,
and cook for 2 minutes, until smooth
and thickened. Remove from the heat
and stir in the lemon zest and butter.
Cool slightly then add the egg yolks
and beat well. Pour the mixture into
the cooked flan case and bake in the
oven for 15 minutes.

Meanwhile, make the meringue
topping. Put the egg whites and salt
in a large bowl. Whisk until stiff, then
add half of the sugar. Continue
whisking until standing in stiff peaks.
Add the remaining sugar and whisk
again. Pile the meringue over the
partly cooked flan, swirling the
surface into peaks. Return to the oven
for a further 15 minutes until the
meringue is beginning to brown.
Serve warm or cold.

Serves 6-8

BLUEBERRY FRANGIPANE FLAN

INGREDIENTS

*85g (3 oz/¹⁄₃ cup) butter, plus extra
for greasing*
*1 quantity Rich Sweet Pastry (see
page 95)*
85g (3 oz/¹⁄₃ cup) caster sugar
1 egg, beaten
85g (3 oz/³⁄₄ cup) ground almonds
few drops of almond essence
25g (1 oz/2 tablespoons) plain flour
225g (8 oz/1¹⁄₂ cups) blueberries
*To serve: icing sugar, crème fraîche
or ice cream*

METHOD

Preparation time: 25 minutes

Preheat the oven to 200° C/400° F/ Gas 6. Use a little butter to grease a 23 cm (9 inch) fluted flan tin. On a lightly floured surface, roll out the pastry and use to line the prepared tin. Lightly prick the base and chill for 15 minutes. Line the pastry case with kitchen or greaseproof paper and fill with baking beans. Bake blind in the oven for 10 minutes then remove the paper and baking beans and return to the oven for a further 5 minutes to cook the base. Reduce the oven temperature to 180° C/350° F/Gas 4.

To make the frangipane filling: in a large bowl beat together the butter and sugar until pale and fluffy then beat in the egg. Fold in the ground almonds, almond essence and flour.

Spoon half of the frangipane filling into the pastry and smooth the surface. Sprinkle the blueberries over and then spread the remaining filling mixture over the fruit. Bake in the oven for 35-40 minutes until the filling is firm and light golden brown. Serve the flan warm, dusted with a little icing sugar, with crème fraîche or ice cream.

Serves 6

INGREDIENTS

350g (12 oz/1½ cups) bought sweet
  shortcrust pastry
300 ml (½ pint/1¾ cups) single
  (light) cream
5 tablespoons milk
25g (1 oz/2 tablespoons) caster
  sugar
2 eggs
1 egg yolk
1 teaspoon vanilla essence
225g (8 oz/1½ cups) raspberries

METHOD

Preparation time: 25 minutes

Preheat the oven to 220° C/425° F/
Gas 7. On a floured surface roll out
the pastry and use to line six 10 cm
(4 inch) tartlet tins. Prick the bases
all over with a fork and chill for 10-15
minutes. Bake the tartlet cases blind
in the oven for 10 minutes. Reduce
the oven temperature to 190° C/
375° F/Gas 5.

Meanwhile, put the cream and milk in
a small saucepan. Heat gently and
then add the sugar. Stir until the
sugar has dissolved. Do not allow the
mixture to boil.

In a medium bowl beat the eggs and
egg yolk. Add the hot cream, beating
constantly. Strain the mixture into a
measuring jug. Divide the custard
between the prepared tartlet cases
and add raspberries to each. Bake in
the oven for about 25 minutes or until
lightly set. Serve warm or cool.

Serves 6

FILO TARTLETS WITH SUMMER FRUITS

INGREDIENTS

about 6 sheets filo pastry
55g (2 oz/¼ cup) butter, melted
4 teaspoons strawberry, cherry or
* raspberry conserve*
175g (6 oz/¾ cup) crème fraîche
2 tablespoons icing sugar, plus extra
* for dusting*
few drops vanilla essence
350g (12 oz/2 cups) mixed summer
* fruits, eg red or white currants,*
* strawberries, raspberries,*
* blueberries, cherries*
To decorate: fruit leaves or scented
* geranium leaves*

METHOD   Preparation time: 20-25 minutes

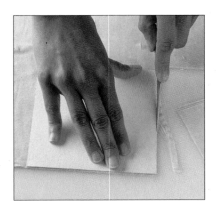

Preheat the oven to 200° C/400° F/ Gas 6. Cut the pastry into twelve 13 cm (5 inch) squares. Arrangé in a pile and cover with a clean damp cloth to prevent drying out. Brush a little of the melted butter round the insides of four 10 cm (4 inch) tartlet tins or individual deep Yorkshire pudding tins.

Brush the filo squares, one at a time, with butter, layering 3 squares in each tin to make attractive, softly fluted tartlet cases. Place on a baking sheet and bake in the oven for 10-15 minutes until golden brown. Carefully remove the tartlet cases from the tins and transfer to a wire rack to cool. Just before serving, place the tartlet cases on four individual serving plates. Put a spoonful of fruit conserve in the base of each.

In a small bowl mix together the crème fraîche, icing sugar and vanilla essence. Divide between the filo tartlets and arrange the fruits on top. Dust lightly with a little icing sugar. Decorate the tartlets with fruit leaves or scented geranium leaves.

VARIATION
Fill the tartlets with good quality bought ice cream or sorbet (to save time) and fresh fruits.

Serves 4

91

RICOTTA CHEESECAKE

INGREDIENTS

55g (2 oz/¼ cup) butter, plus extra
   for greasing
25g (1 oz/2 tablespoons) walnuts
115g (4 oz/½ cup) amaretti biscuits
3 teaspoons powdered gelatine
finely grated rind juice and, 1 lemon
350g (12 oz/1½ cups) ricotta cheese
55g (2 oz/¼ cup) caster sugar
2 eggs, separated
300 ml (½ pint/1¼ cups) single
   (light) cream
To decorate:
1 large ripe peach or nectarine
4 tablespoons redcurrant jelly

METHOD   **Preparation time:** 30 minutes

Use a little butter to grease a 20 cm (8 inch) loose-bottomed cake tin. Put the walnuts and amaretti biscuits in a food processor or blender and process until they form fine crumbs. Melt the butter in a saucepan and add the biscuit mixture. Mix together well. Press the mixture over the base of the prepared cake tin. Chill while preparing the cheese mixture. In a small bowl or cup soak the gelatine in the lemon juice, then stand in a pan of hot water and stir until dissolved.

Put the ricotta in a large bowl with the lemon rind, sugar, egg yolks and cream. Whisk until smooth. Add the gelatine mixture and whisk again. In a clean bowl whisk the egg whites until stiff. Using a large metal spoon fold into the cheese mixture. Spoon over the biscuit base and chill until set (for at least 2 hours).

Remove the cheesecake from the tin and transfer to a serving plate. To decorate, halve and stone the peach or nectarine and slice thinly. Arrange on top of the cheesecake. Gently melt the redcurrant jelly in a small pan. Cool slightly and spoon over the fruit to glaze.

Serves 6

INGREDIENTS

375g (13 oz/1½ cups) frozen sweet
  shortcrust pastry, defrosted
Filling:
finely grated zest and juice of 4
  lemons
3 eggs
1 egg yolk
115g (4 oz/½ cup) caster sugar
150 ml (¼ pint/⅔ cup) double
  (thick) cream
Topping:
3 lemons
175g (6 oz/⅔ cups) caster sugar
To serve: single (light) cream

METHOD

Preparation time: 30 minutes

Preheat the oven to 220° C/425° F/ Gas 7. Oil a 23 cm (9 inch) fluted flan tin. On a lightly floured surface roll out the pastry and use to line the prepared flan tin. Chill for 20 minutes. Line the tart shell with kitchen or greaseproof paper and fill with baking beans. Bake blind in the oven for 10 minutes and then remove the paper and baking beans and return to the oven for 5 minutes to cook the base. Reduce the oven temperature to 160° C/325° F/Gas 3.

Meanwhile, prepare the filling: in a large jug or bowl whisk together all the ingredients until smooth and well blended. Pour into the tart shell and bake in the oven for 45-50 minutes or until set. Remove from the oven and leave to cool in the tin. To make the topping: using a small sharp knife, peel the lemons removing all the white pith. Thinly slice the lemons. Put the sugar in a saucepan with 150 ml (¼ pint/⅔ cup) cold water. Heat gently, stirring constantly until the sugar has completely dissolved.

Add the lemon slices to the pan and bring to the boil. Boil for 30 seconds then remove from the heat. Using a slotted spoon, carefully lift out the lemon slices. Arrange them on the top of the tart. Bring the syrup back to boiling point and boil steadily for 1 minute. Spoon the syrup over the tart and cool completely before removing from the tin. Serve the tart cold, but not chilled, with single (light) cream.

Serves 6

TARTE FRANÇAISE

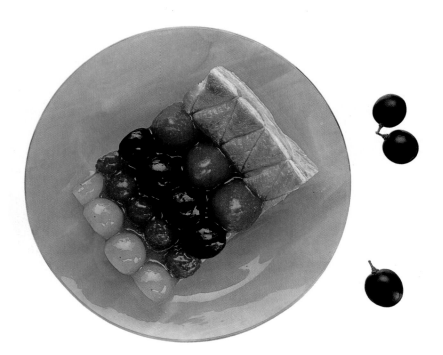

INGREDIENTS

*375g (13 oz/1½ cups) frozen puff
  pastry, defrosted
1 egg yolk mixed with 1 teaspoon
  water
Apricot glaze:
6 tablespoons apricot jam
4 teaspoons lemon juice
Fruit filling:
about 150g (5 oz/1 cup) small
  strawberries
115g (4 oz/1 cup) black grapes,
  seeded
115g (4 oz/1 cup) green grapes,
  seeded
115g (4 oz/1 cup) raspberries
To serve: lightly whipped cream or
  crème fraîche*

METHOD

Preparation time: 25 minutes

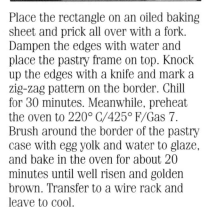

On a lightly floured surface roll out
the pastry to form a rectangle about
30 x 20 cm (12 x 8 inches). Lightly
dust the surface of the pastry with
flour and fold lengthwise in half.
Keeping the folded edge of pastry
intact, cut out a rectangle, leaving a
3.5cm (1½ inch) border to give a
frame. Open out the centre piece and
roll out to match the size of the pastry
frame.

Place the rectangle on an oiled baking
sheet and prick all over with a fork.
Dampen the edges with water and
place the pastry frame on top. Knock
up the edges with a knife and mark a
zig-zag pattern on the border. Chill
for 30 minutes. Meanwhile, preheat
the oven to 220° C/425° F/Gas 7.
Brush around the border of the pastry
case with egg yolk and water to glaze,
and bake in the oven for about 20
minutes until well risen and golden
brown. Transfer to a wire rack and
leave to cool.

In a small pan, gently heat the apricot
jam with the lemon juice, stirring until
melted. Sieve and keep warm. Brush
a little over the base of the pastry
case. Arrange the fruit in rows in the
pastry case and brush generously
with the remaining apricot glaze.
Leave to set. Serve with lightly
whipped cream or crème fraîche.

Serves 6

NORMANDY APPLE FLAN

INGREDIENTS

Rich sweet pastry:
150g (5 oz/²/₃ cups) plain flour
85g (3 oz/¹/₃ cup) butter, cut into
* pieces*
45g (1¹/₂ oz/3 tablespoons) caster
* sugar*
2 egg yolks
Filling:
675g (1¹/₂ lb/6 cups) dessert apples
300 ml (¹/₂ pint/1¹/₄ cups) single
* (light) cream*
2 egg yolks
¹/₂ teaspoon vanilla essence
70g (2¹/₂ oz/¹/₄ cup) caster sugar
To serve: single (light) cream

METHOD

Preparation time: 30 minutes

To make the rich sweet pastry: sieve the flour into a large bowl. Rub in the butter. Stir in the sugar. Add the egg yolks and using a palette knife, mix to a firm dough. Knead lightly until smooth, then wrap in clingfilm and chill for 20 minutes. Lightly oil a fluted 23 cm (9 inch) flan ring or tin. Turn the dough on to a lightly floured surface and roll out. Use to line the prepared flan ring. Chill for a further 20 minutes.

Preheat the oven to 190° C/375° F/ Gas 5. To make the filling: peel, core and thinly slice the apples. Arrange them in the flan case finishing with an attractive overlapping layer. In a bowl or jug beat together the cream, egg yolks, vanilla essence and all but 2 tablespoons of the sugar. Pour over the apples and bake the flan in the centre of the oven for 30 minutes.

Lower the oven temperature to 180℃/ 350° F/Gas 4 and sprinkle the remaining sugar over the flan. Return to the oven for 25-30 minutes until the apples are tender and lightly browned. Allow to cool slightly before removing the flan from the tin. Serve warm or cold with single (light) cream.

Serves 6-8